PENGUIN BOOKS

RIGHTEOUS

Lauren Sandler is the Life Editor of *Salon*. She has written about cultural politics for numerous newspapers and magazines, including the *Atlantic Monthly*, the *New York Times*, the *Los Angeles Times*, and has been featured on National Public Radio. She lives in Brooklyn.

Praise for *Righteous*

"Sandler has an old-fashioned reporter's knack for telling details. Her portraits of the leaders of this movement are sharp and often hilarious. . . . Sandler clearly has a talent for getting people to open up about their beliefs, and she has enough respect for her subjects that she rarely indulges in caricatures. Sandler is at her best when she documents the longing this generation feels for certainty, community, and purpose. Sandler's book is an intriguing journey into a burgeoning and often contradictory phenomenon."
—*The Washington Post*

"While always being forthright about being at odds with the worldview of the young Evangelicals she tracks, [Sandler] writes with keen insight and empathy about those involved in a range of youth ministries."
—*The Christian Science Monitor*

"You will find Sandler's book worth every penny. It is a siren call for all people of faith, or no faith, who find fundamentalism unsettling. . . . Yet this is not a total bash book. Despite her obvious misgivings, Sandler acknowledges a certain admiration, even warmth, for many of the young men and women she encountered along the way."
—*The San Diego Union-Tribune*

"[Sandler's] writing is crisp and some of her best work comes when she seems, like the old hymn, to be almost persuaded to join the fold."
—*The Hartford Courant*

"Sandler . . . offers the most interesting conclusion: a call for the return of wonder, fellowship, and authenticity to the secular public sphere."
—*The Atlantic Monthly*

"Lauren Sandler obliterates the naive and complacent hope that keeps most secularists and religious moderates sleeping peacefully each night—the hope that, in twenty-first century America, the young know better than to adopt the lunatic religious certainties of a prior age. The young do not know better. In their schools, skate parks, rock concerts, and in the ranks of our nation's military, our children are gleefully preparing a bright future of ignorance and religious fascism for us all. If you have any doubt that there is a culture war that must be waged and won by secularists in America, read this book."
—Sam Harris, author of *The End of Faith* and *Letter to a Christian Nation*

"Shrewd perception combined with spirited writing in *Righteous*, Lauren Sandler's cross-country portrait of the right-wing Christian youth movements—from hip-hop capitalists to Air Force Academy Armageddon believers—whom she labels the Disciple Generation, this because they seek to submerge themselves in faith and belief. In contrast to the 1960s, the new youthful statement of tattoos, earrings and rock music now combines with the quasi-military recruitment, flags, mass meetings and the moral fundamentalism of Jerry Falwell and abortion clinic attackers. Sandler believes a secular Great Awakening is needed to counteract this tide, and parents and young people alike can begin by reading her frightening portrait."

—Kevin Phillips, bestselling author of *American Dynasty* and *American Theocracy*

"It is no easy thing to enter into the world of the young Evangelicals, to feel deeply their alienation, to breathe their air and share their electric conviction that they are the rising counterculture against an empty world. Lauren Sandler has done it, and done it with an effervescence and honesty that make her travels in Disciple America jump off the page."

—Todd Gitlin, professor of journalism and sociology, Columbia University, and author of *The Intellectuals and the Flag*

"At once controversial, critical, blasphemous and compassionate, *Righteous* offers a compelling journey into a growing youth subculture typically dismissed by urban intellectuals. Sandler has written a provocative and illuminating portrait of young people desperately seeking meaning, community and love in an empty, often terrifying social landscape. Evangelical youth—the Disciple Generation—are a generation rising, and we do need to pay attention."

—Dr. Donna Gaines, sociologist and author of *Teenage Wasteland: Suburbia's Dead End Kids* and *A Misfit's Manifesto: The Spiritual Journey of a Rock & Roll Heart*

"Lauren Sandler has traveled among the believers and returned with a story that alarms, informs, and enlightens. She reveals the rise of a fundamentalist-style youth movement that has replaced faith with closed-minded certainty and is frighteningly cultlike. Read this book and you will understand this Disciple Generation and the challenge it poses to a civil society."

—Michael D'Antonio, former *Newsday* religion writer and author of *Fall From Grace* and *Heaven on Earth*

"*Righteous* is a lively, probing account of today's fresh, sometimes bizarre subcultures of American Evangelism. Both the terms 'alternative' and 'evangelical' will mean something new to you after this book. Sandler's conclusions are important: These kids have been forgotten by their original social worlds, by secular organizations and even by Left-Liberal causes. In a cold new world, getting saved can now seem like a young American's only source of community and warmth."

—Alissa Quart, author of *Hothouse Kids: The Dilemma of the Gifted Child*

righteous

Dispatches from the
Evangelical Youth Movement

LAUREN SANDLER

Penguin Books

PENGUIN BOOKS

Published by the Penguin Group
Penguin Group (USA) Inc., 375 Hudson Street, New York, New York 10014, U.S.A.
Penguin Group (Canada), 90 Eglinton Avenue East, Suite 700, Toronto,
Ontario, Canada M4P 2Y3 (a division of Pearson Penguin Canada Inc.)
Penguin Books Ltd, 80 Strand, London WC2R 0RL, England
Penguin Ireland, 25 St Stephen's Green, Dublin 2, Ireland
(a division of Penguin Books Ltd)
Penguin Group (Australia), 250 Camberwell Road, Camberwell,
Victoria 3124, Australia (a division of Pearson Australia Group Pty Ltd)
Penguin Books India Pvt Ltd, 11 Community Centre,
Panchsheel Park, New Delhi – 110 017, India
Penguin Group (NZ), 67 Apollo Drive, Rosedale, North Shore 0745,
Auckland, New Zealand (a division of Pearson New Zealand Ltd)
Penguin Books (South Africa) (Pty) Ltd, 24 Sturdee Avenue,
Rosebank, Johannesburg 2196, South Africa

Penguin Books Ltd, Registered Offices:
80 Strand, London WC2R 0RL, England

First published in the United States of America by Viking Penguin,
a member of Penguin Group (USA) Inc. 2006
Published in Penguin Books 2007

10   9   8   7   6   5   4   3   2

Photographs by Justin Lane

ISBN 0-670-03791-5 (hc.)
ISBN 978-0-14-311237-2 (pbk.)
CIP data available

Printed in the United States of America
Set in Janson Text   Designed by Spring Hoteling

To my parents, for everything.

To my parents, for everything

Why does this generation seek a sign?
Assuredly, I say to you, no sign will be
given to this generation.

—Mark 8:12

You Will Know Them

by Their Numbers

1. Age of born-again Christians most likely to have engaged in evangelical behavior in 2004: 18-to-20-year-olds (88 percent)
2. Percentage of high school students who support prayer in public school: 84
3. Percentage greater than Americans overall: 8
4. Percentage of entering college freshmen who attend church: 81
5. Percentage greater than Americans overall: 15
6. Percentage points by which highly religiously engaged college freshmen are more likely than those with low religious engagement to

   - Favor increasing military spending: 14
   - Support giving colleges the right to ban extreme speakers: 15
   - Support laws that prohibit homosexual relationships: 37

7. Percentage increase in total enrollment for all public four-year colleges and universities from 1990 to 2004: 12:8

8. Percentage increase in enrollment at the 102 campuses that are members of the Council for Christian Colleges and Universities, a group that works to advance Christ-centered higher education by relating scholarship and service to "biblical truth": 70.6

9. Number of U.S. public school districts that have adopted a class in which the Bible is the primary textbook: 301

10. Percentage of Americans who say that God created life on earth: 78

11. Number of scientists with accepted academic credentials in earth or life science who give credence to creation science: 700 of 480,000

12. Increase in sales of religious music from 1989 to 2005: 318 percent

13. Estimated number of Christian music festivals held in the summer of 2000 attended by more than 5,000 youths: 5

14. Estimated number of Christian music festivals held in the summer of 2005 attended by over 5,000 youths: 35

15. Growth of congregants at Mars Hill Church, a youth-led conservative church in Seattle, from 1998 to 2005: 150 to 3,500

16. Projected number of congregants in 2010: 10,000

17. Percentage of the estimated 98 million adult born-again Christians who say they made their commitment to Christ before their eighteenth birthday: 64

18. Percentage of Americans who think liberals have gone too far to keep religion out of schools and government: 67

19. Percentage of Americans who believe that the Bible is the actual Word of God and should be taken literally: 32

See pages 251–252 for Sources.

CONTENTS

———

Contents

You'll Feel Lead

Heather Erickson was an aggressively normal high school student—pretty but not stunning, smart but not brilliant, flirtatious but not promiscuous—a blond drum major with a head for business from a nice middle-class Virginia family. Average grades. Average height. Average problems.

During her senior year Heather stopped making out with boys at parties and set her sights on one guy. Brian was solid boyfriend material—a marine a couple of years older than she was. Even though Heather had toyed with the notion of saving her virginity for marriage, she decided after much deliberation to sleep with him. She was in love. Then Brian stopped calling, but not for your typical commitment-phobe reasons: he had been called up for duty in Iraq, and he was terrified that he was going to find himself at the wrong end of an improvised explosive device, limbless and bleeding to death, the only thought in his fading mind that he had ruined Heather's life by signing up and getting himself killed.

Heather must have redialed Brian's number a thousand times trying to convince him to talk to her so she could change his mind, but eventually she gave up and crawled under her covers to sob for weeks. She wasn't pregnant, drug-addicted, or suicidal; she was just heartbroken. Desperate to crack Heather's depression, her mother bought tickets for an event called Acquire the Fire at the Richmond Coliseum that promised loud bands, a state-of-the-art light show, engaging theatrical performances, and a mass of teenagers gathered to focus on something other than boys and beer. Mildly intrigued and dying for distraction, Heather splashed water on her face and drove into town with her sister to check out the show.

Once inside the stadium, what Heather saw overwhelmed her: ten thousand teens rocking out to catchy power pop, their hands raised to the domed roof, their eyes closed, their faces ebullient. The band was, indeed, loud, and the lights were impressive, but most rapturous of all was the notion that this giant gathering was focused on a single purpose, and it had nothing to do with getting laid or getting dumped. The lyrics on giant prompters framing the stage proclaimed what they were there for: the magnificent, unifying, unconditional love of Jesus Christ.

Heather was hungry for any love to fill her empty, battered heart. Like millions of other teens nationwide who have passed through the doors of an Acquire the Fire revival, she was happy to sing along, her defenses loosened by the music and the crowd's emotion. During a break in the music, a skit about peer pressure seemed to speak directly to her experience at school and with Brian. Suddenly, she felt understood. After the lineup of speakers promised salvation from loneliness and doubt, she finally felt her chest swell with hope.

But Heather's salvation required a bargain: to gain Christ's love, she would have to accept that she had sinned against God by soiling her virgin body with sex, drinking to excess, disrespecting her parents, and by living out a host of normal teenage behaviors. Suddenly shocked by her own impurity, Heather began to cry. Through her deepening sobs, she heard someone from the stage invite the audience to accept Christ as their savior by walking toward one of the giant crosses scattered throughout the stadium, each lit up like a beacon.

Heather felt an invisible force pull her from her seat and lead her down to the nearest cross, where she crumpled into a tearful heap. Then she felt a gentle hand resting on her shoulder. A girl with kind eyes leaned down to ask her if she could pray for her. Heather nodded; she was crying too hard to speak. She wept harder when she heard the words that were whispered in her ear, uncanny words her friends had failed to provide in her time of ordinary sadness, words of deliverance from her pain. This utter stranger prayed to liberate her from the prison of her sins of vanity and lust. "It was like she saw through me," Heather told me. "She was an angel from God. I surrendered everything right then."

When I met Heather a year had passed since she had given her body and soul over to the feeling that had converted her that night. Every aspect of her life was ruled and defined by her newfound faith. In marked contrast, my three decades on this earth have been something of a liberal cliché. An unrepentant Jewish atheist, I was raised in Harvard Square, and have long been registered to vote in New York. To me, the Bible is essentially a game of telephone: a number of word-of-mouth accounts that took hundreds of years to be recorded on paper. But Heather didn't seem to care about my beliefs, politics, or secular lifestyle, all of which she's been trained to wage war against. She didn't want to talk to me about my pro-choice politics, or my support of gay marriage, or, as she might see it, my guaranteed eternity in hell. She just wanted to ask me about losing my virginity in high school, my runaround days in college, my breakup dramas and wedding vows; she wanted to dish, to relate, to force an emotional connection through whispered secrets.

Heather tells me her hunger for connection is commonplace within her generation. Most young Christians I've met agree. They say they feel abandoned by an overwhelming world that they describe as being hollow, destructive—even evil. They yearn for belonging within communities that exist apart from the unrelenting challenges of secular life. What they crave can be satisfied only in their "personal relationship with Jesus Christ," they say, and in the regiments of an army that gains strength every day, fighting in his name.

I ventured out on the American road to seek insight into what I suspected was a mounting Evangelical youth movement. My travels were a journalist's journey—I wanted to bear witness to our new Christian cavalry. Crisscrossing the country, I slept on church floors, camped out with activists, and endured more ecstatic testimonies than I care to remember, lingering and listening in places where I was wanted and where I wasn't. I was welcomed into circles of upright soldiers and activist vegans, tattooed dropouts and collegiate nerds, all united in the same battle for Jesus Christ. I smelled the sourness of teen sweat in frenzied megachurches, broke bread in young couples' homes, and, every Sunday, heard pastors call me the enemy.

Within this movement, I discovered something as old as America itself, and as terrifying and alluring as anything Orwell predicted; something that is at once political, emotional, deeply anti-intellectual, and more galvanized than I ever imagined. I call this population of fierce young Evangelicals the Disciple Generation. And I believe its rapid expansion is the secular world's own damn fault.

The Disciple Generation is an ever-growing population of people ages fifteen to thirty-five who are equally obsessed with Christ and with culture as a means to an Evangelical end. People within this age bracket are defined by a shared culture, whether Christian or secular: if you own an iPod, know Green Day is a band and not a Nader rally, and ever considered getting a tattoo, you're probably within the boundary. This is an age group whose transgressive actions—regardless of faith or demographic, whether in the form of an inked bicep, high school detention, or a fundamentalist credo—are easily slapped with the label of rebellion. But for Christians within this generation, behavior and beliefs are unlike those of any archetypal rebellion that has come before.

For every member of the Disciple Generation I've met who was raised secular in a car or a commune, or had a lesbian mom or a pothead dad, I've met plenty more who grew up in traditional Christian homes, whether that affiliation took the form of an occasional Sunday service or a father who was an active church elder. There's a three-piece suit for every freshly shaved mohawk in this subculture. Yet wherever they began their individual walk with Christ, and however they choose to outwardly identify themselves within the subculture, members of this movement all talk about a meaningless and bankrupt society; a world that offers no anodyne culture outside their faith. Their lives are in fact a criticism of our own. This youth movement isn't one that merely defines itself against its parents' generation; it exists in opposition to all culture and history that excludes Evangelicalism.

These new disciples have ripped down their parents' white steeples and torn apart the lumber to build a half-pipe. Christian youth is deinstitutionalizing the American church for the first time in about four hundred years. This Evangelical movement isn't just about internally held principles, it's a matter of lifestyle. Young Evangelicals look so similar to denizens of every other strain of youth culture that, aside from their religious tattoos, the difference between them and the unsaved is invisible. Shattering the perceived blue state–red state dichotomy, epicenters of this Evangelical movement are swelling madly in the leftist zip codes of cities like Boston and Portland. In rural Illinois, a guy in a T-shirt with BODY PIERCING SAVED MY LIFE on the front and an image of the stigmata on the back told me that he had no doubt that Jesus would come back fronting a hard-core band. In Denver, a crowd of skate punks disagreed—the Lord was surely returning with a skateboard in hand. In Seattle, a father-to-be in his early twenties grinned as he described the Christian world his child would be born into. "It's gotten to the point that when I see someone covered in great tattoos, I assume they're Christian," he told me. "This isn't about imagining the future for us. We're already here. This is already ours."

Mainstream radio plays Christian indie pop. At high schools across the country the in crowd proselytizes to the out crowd. A majority of teens and twenty-somethings, many of whom don't even self-identify as born-again, scoff at the very notion of evolution, preferring instead to believe that something as astonishing as human life must surely be the plan of an intelligent designer. The Evangelical culture is in place, and it's expanding every day to swallow a generation whole.

In case this world is unfamiliar to you, to be an Evangelical Christian, you typically need to believe that the Bible is the infallible Word of God; you've got to be game to save souls; and you usually need to have some sort of crisis conversion. That's the moment when your heart opens to God and you accept Jesus Christ as your personal savior. That's when you commit your life to absolutism.

I have heard people tell me countless times that in their moment of conversion they felt a sense of *brokenness* that could be fixed only by faith, a profound despair that begs for comfort in the authority of the divine and the promise of salvation. At the heart of this emerging movement is the horror of uncertainty—the stomach-clenching experience of looking outward at a world that guarantees neither safety nor peace, and looking inward into a personal realm that promises neither clarity nor surety. "Nothing feels familiar anymore, or *certain*," a pastor told me, echoing the sentiments of hundreds of Christian kids I've met. "We've pushed through nearly every boundary or taboo," he said.

As the globe shrinks in the Internet age, information overwhelms, and the choices one may make—what to wear, watch, study, and believe—increase exponentially, offering no certainty at all. *What's the right answer?* is no longer a viable question in a relative world that has long outgrown its moral guideposts. Ever since the industrial revolution, people have experienced the paralyzing angst of modernity; today it has spun out of control, resulting in a crisis for this generation. To a few kids I've met, such a boundless world is freeing, but most seem to seek protection from a ubiquitous onslaught of infinite information. We have been liberated from the limits of the past: nothing today is what it was—not war, not sex, not family. The result is a population that wants liberation *from* liberation.

A complicated world gives rise to an extraordinary yearning for the literal. In response to the previously incomprehensible broadness of the globe, perspectives narrow, absolutes reign. People escape into absolutism the way they retreated into fallout shelters during the Cold War, erecting concrete barriers to blind and protect themselves from what they imagine lurking outside. If you believe God created your life with a purpose, you are warmed against the cold, steely concept that the universe is infinite and random. And if you can derive that purpose from a book that points the way to heaven, then what can secularists possibly offer as a better guiding light through the chaos?

It's not surprising that our country has ended up in this morass of fundamentalism. We've been careening toward this state of anti-intellectualism since the *Mayflower* dropped anchor; the lure of absolutism is our great and tragic inevitability. Emigrants from Europe fled a land ruled by aristocrats in book-lined, gilded drawing rooms to build a new world from dirt and timber with their bare hands. These ideas lay the groundwork of our democratic antielitism, but their flip side is a dangerous one. This land was a wilderness conquered in the name of religious fervor, and its subsequent nation was built on a foundation of zeal. Our history is one of frequent spells of religious revivals tailored to the emotions and needs of the day; our elections bought and sold on how voters "feel" about a candidate regardless of his or her record.

This Evangelical youth movement is at its heart an American phenomenon. Each conversion means something incomparably formidable and intense to the individual, but the millions of conversions taken in the aggregate add up to a collective indictment of our contemporary society. To young Evangelicals, our secular world is devoid of the type of love they seek, not parental love or fraternal love or even erotic love, but an even bigger love—a love called agape.

Agape is a love without expected reciprocation, judgment, or need. It's a concept so unusual in modern society that we have no word for it, save for this ancient Greek term that remains in the Bible. When Christians describe God's love for his children this is the word they invoke, a love so powerful one is moved to proclaim it on car bumpers and coffee mugs. Agape is what Christianity promises, and what good Christians—I daresay *real* Christians—attempt to deliver (and receive) in their daily lives. Hand in hand with certainty, agape is what this generation longs for today—a love that will soothe the pain of breakups and breakouts, heal the wounds from shattered families, make bearable the awareness that we are each a solitary speck in an illimitable world. It's the emotion that secularism, enraptured by its logic and empiricism, refuses to engage.

My journey across the country and through the Evangelical youth movement began after George Bush's bewildering re-election knocked the air from my lungs and the hope from my heart. "Values voters," so many televised faces told us, had championed their beliefs at the polls while Democrats—those voters whose values have historically been actualized in committing their tax dollars to eradicate poverty and improve education, not in parroting their pastors' rhetoric—failed to galvanize a change. The low turnout among young voters was once again a reminder of our apolitical age, and our distance from the civil rights marches on Washington and rage on display at the 1968 Democratic Convention in Chicago. But nowhere to be found was a discussion of the youth component of those "values voters"—the myriad Christians I had met since the nineties at skate parks and punk clubs.

The relative silence about this evolving youth movement is especially menacing to me when regarded from the broad vantage of history. It seems to me that the growth of the Disciple Generation, a movement of staggering demographic diversity united by an intensely shared faith, suggests we've arrived at a significant precipice. We are poised before the next Great Awakening in American history. And considering this nation's metastasizing anti-intellectualism, the crumbling wall between church and state, and the relative absence of community and meaning in the secular world, I've got news for you: this awakening ain't so great.

Great Awakenings are periods of mass revivals that convert huge numbers of people to Christianity, shaping not just this nation's foundations of faith, but also our culture and politics. The First Great Awakening occurred from about 1730 to 1760, setting every community ablaze with religion. Between 1800 and 1830, in the tumult of young nationhood, Americans bereft of a clear national identity and a dependable civil structure found solidity in Christianity, and gave rise to the Second Great Awakening. Some historians regard the mass conversions of 1890 to 1920 as another Great Awakening—during which religious fervor spread in response to the turmoil set off by industrialization and immigration—which once again redefined the country and the lives of its citizens.

Awakenings grow out of a historical moment in which social behavior has begun to deviate from traditional norms; widespread cultural disorientation and anxiety result from a time of opposing messages. A religious revival takes root, growing underground throughout the nation, eventually transforming the way we live. Identity shifts and calcifies at an accelerated pace. New myths are born, and codes of behavior and values are set. In those eras, as now, Americans are defined and redefined.

Each awakening in its early stages features religious leaders addressing the masses with a fervent call to old values, old habits, and that old-time religion. In our time, the initial wave of leaders included Billy Graham, Jerry Falwell, and anyone who spent the eighties weeping and pleading for cash on television. This generation of leaders looked for scapegoats for society's ills and politicized their followers against them—what political scientist Jean Hardisty has termed "mobilizing resentment." Communists, Soviet and otherwise, were the first targets in this cycle; these days Christians have the Middle East and gay America to rail against, thereby asserting their moral and political authority in a nation weak on dissent.

But the reach of such old-school leaders is limited. In every case and every century, a full awakening can never spread in their hands alone. Their backward-looking philosophy fails to motivate a new generation, to whom their doctrine and culture feels irrelevant. They want to reverse the flow of a river, not change its course. To reach a nation, a population needs to be redirected away from old institutions toward a radical new culture. An awakening entails young people reinventing traditional rituals, making the faith of their forefathers their own. This isn't just an observation on the MTV age—it's been the final stage of every awakening before a national transformation is complete. To hit critical mass, it takes a youth movement.

On the morning of September 11, 2001, I stood on the Brooklyn Promenade watching the World Trade Center collapse across the East River. As I crossed over the Brooklyn Bridge toward Manhattan, interviewing ash-covered survivors for the *Los Angeles Times*, I had an instant of removal from the tragedy occurring before me. Like many other people staring at our scarred and smoking skyline that morning, I reflected on how this cataclysm might change forever how people would see the world. Amid all the other things to consider—fear and love and foreign policy and jihad—it occurred to me that we might finally have something to unite this fragmented country, something to rally against together, a cohesion not seen since the sixties. Watching two strangers brush dust off each other's sunken shoulders, I had a peculiar flash of optimism about the future and a condemnation of the recent past. I thought: *Surely this will crack through our national disinterest. This crisis will spawn a youth movement and a culture that will shake our country to its self-consumed core.*

It took me a year or two to realize that the ideological unity of the sixties had already arrived. It's hard to imagine Acquire the Fire's totalitarian tableaux evincing any connection to the decade of free love and free thinking, but this movement is far more than a series of massive revivals. In the Disciple Generation, young Evangelicals connect, organize, and reside within a movement that both exists on an intimate grassroots level and super-sized in stadium events. The sixties have been both resurrected and subverted in every rock-festival activist and road-trip missionary; their hipster home Bible studies and MySpace forums operate as modern-day consciousness groups. They've infused youth culture with meaning and dissent, built intentional communities, and imagined their destiny.

Of course, this counterculture is not organized to perpetuate the politics of the sixties. Feminism, sexual freedom, secular liberalism: all these words are profanity to the Disciple Generation. The sixties counterculture was united against a mendacious government and the military that carried out its policy overseas, whereas this movement counts the president as one of its own, and views the military as a mission tool. In the new Christian counterculture, dreadlocks ally with buzz cuts, organizing against anything that challenges the perceived literal perfection of the Bible: the notion of "inerrancy," which means that every word of the Bible is considered to be absolute truth. Christians perceive threats to this notion everywhere—in the media, the public school system, and the non-Christian nations around the globe. Some respond by following the extraordinary model of Jesus' love, others become borderline fascists, and many fall in between. All of them are revolutionaries filling the vacuum abandoned by the left when it moved on from the culture it pioneered for a life less radical.

Plenty of sixties survivors have noted that the New Left failed to create lasting systemic change in the arena of politics, but none could dispute that the era forever altered our nation's experience of culture. In its music married to ideology, experiments in intentional living, and activist cool, the counterculture became a legacy to be poached by its counter-revolutionaries. Its techniques and expressions, which at the time seemed so inextricable from its politics, became an organizing model for its ideological opposite. In these sixties-style modes, Evangelicalism has rushed in to pervade nearly every corner of our society.

Little did the left know back then that it was creating a

blueprint for the right, and little does it know that a strange doppelganger of that movement exists today. Tattoos have replaced love beads, skater-punk and hip-hop have replaced folk and psychedelic rock, and the down-and-dirty politics of the far right have replaced the visionary idealism of the New Left. But the infrastructure of the new Great Awakening is a model that's pure sixties, organizing and inspiring through youth culture, active and intense community groups, and the melding of music and meaning, pop and politics.

Like nothing else, shared culture is an opportunity for people to connect and gain one another's trust. Culture—your favorite music, sport, pastime, style, you name it—presents an opening for evangelism. Once bonds are forged over a beloved band or football team, then the Evangelical "message" can work its way into a relationship. It's what an Evangelical novelist I know calls being "sneaky deep." Once the message is heard, a world opens in which God's love, as well as your cultural predilections, provide spiritual isolation from the secular world. It's hard to imagine an aspect of secular culture lacking a Christian counterpart: one can choose from Christian hip-hop ministries, Christian military intelligence classes, or Christian diet groups in this mirror society.

At Acquire the Fire events preppie kids lay hands on pierced Goths and vice versa—literally by the tens of thousands. Unlike any other youth movement in history, at least that I can think of, the Disciple Generation integrates kids across well-defined cultural boundaries in a single unifying bond, a dominant ideology without a dominant aesthetic.

This is a movement fusing young Americans with seemingly opposing identities—drum majors with skaters with Senate aides—in a single faith and with few exceptions, a single politic. Young Evangelicals know what they believe. They *stand* for something; they have a hopeful narrative for human experience, a *big idea* to apply to our times. Christians reach out to people who feel broken and lonely, who desire kinship and purpose, who look for structure and hope, and through their deft organizing efforts and boundless energy, they are amassing their own civilian army.

In the sixties an army of youth took to the streets to battle the injustice poisoning the world and killing its generation. This Christian army likewise sees a wave of destruction crashing over the globe, its own generation at risk. Its war is a culture war. Until secular America strengthens its own front lines by developing strong communities and a culture that uplifts rather than invalidates, this army will have no viable opponent. It aims to destroy everything that it is not. Maintain no illusion: they are wide awake. They are ready.

How does ingenuous, wide-eyed Heather Erickson fit into this alliance of crusaders? Little did she know at the moment of her conversion that she wasn't going to return to her normal teen life, graduate high school, and pack up for college like the rest of her friends. Acquire the Fire isn't just an evening that drops new Christians at Jesus' doorstep and wishes them luck. These revivals demand more than conversion: they are a strategy for hard-line, military-style recruitment into a ministry aptly called Teen Mania, founded by a former addict and runaway named Ron Luce. Heather put her college plans on hold, deferring from Virginia Tech to become a full-time Christian soldier at Luce's command.

Luce's West Point is the Honor Academy, a yearlong training program for Christian soldiers at the Teen Mania east Texas campus, where the security is high, the grounds are immaculately manicured, and the students run everything from the development office to the cafeteria. Heather signed up the day after she was born again at the Richmond Coliseum; that sweet girl who prayed with her had pitched the academy as soon as Heather stopped crying. The enlisted, called interns, defer their first year of college to attend. Dating is verboten—a single kiss guarantees expulsion. Male interns are not allowed to use the Internet unsupervised, should the lure of porn prove irresistible. Female interns attend classes in purity coaching. Silver bands engraved with *Semper Honorabilis*—"Always Honorable"—are given out and expected to be worn for life.

The year begins with the Gauntlet, a ceremony replete with medieval-style sword rituals. Honor Academy demands constant work, religious education, and prayer. Breaks come in the form of weekends called Life Transforming Experiences, when interns fast and pray silently for two or three days, or Emotionally Stretching Opportunities of a Lifetime, when they undergo army-style physical training. These ESOLs, as they are known, include Persecution Training courses in which interns are allowed little sleep or food, and run drills like crawling through sandy trenches and watery pits behind a team leader bearing a huge cross—literally—while facilitators representing the secular sphere verbally abuse them and try to shake their faith in God. "The entire world is against you!" they bellow. "Where is your faith? As a Christian you're all alone!" No maneuvers are too ruthless when it comes to building the perfect salvation army.

Anyone who has attended Acquire the Fire knows what's happening to America just by simple math: Luce is filling stadiums where the Detroit Lions and Washington Redskins have a hard time selling out seats. He has written a book called *Battle Cry for a Generation*, in which he states that one should try a little trick for inspiration, should one's resolve weaken in "battle." "Put a bullet in your pocket," he suggests, "and touch it every time you get those feelings—you'll *feel lead*." Somehow, fondling ammunition hardly suggests the right answer to the question *What would Jesus do?* Luce's Branch Davidian–style training camp and creepy militant motivational tactics may sound like the work of an extremist and marginalized holy roller, but in fact, his supporters include George W. Bush, who in 2003 appointed him as a White House advisor. When Heather shows me the giant framed certificate signed by the president that hangs in Teen Mania's entry hall, she can barely contain her pride. She tells me, her young pink face aglow, "Look at what we're all a part of now."

This is not the story of a youth movement gathering on the horizon. It's already here. And it's growing every day.

1

Fetal Position

It's another sweltering afternoon at Cornerstone, the annual Christian rock festival that draws fifty thousand people to a stretch of Illinois farmland, and the vegans are hungry. In the murky light under the Rock for Life tent, a band sets up onstage while pierced and dreadlocked blondes lay out a buffet of beans and vegetables. Amid the din of guitar tuning, a forum for seventy-odd "progressive" antiabortionists assembles on the matted grass, one of two dozen Rock for Life seminars during this five-day festival—and they're the last people you'd visualize upon hearing the words "single-issue voter."

A microphone passes from grimy hand to hand as the discussion opens with testimony from former members of the left wing. None of these people would consider themselves to be participants in a grassroots *political* movement. There are no politics here, they say, only Christ's love. But now that the Disciple Generation has taken the church outside the meetinghouse and dispersed it throughout an entire lifestyle, there is no differentiation between faith and politics. Faith *is* politics, just as it's everything else to this new wave of believers. It touches every aspect of who you know, where you live, and what you believe—and by engaging the unengageable with a message of love, their outreach is more effective than any other political group I've seen.

A young man with waist-length dreads suspends his busywork knotting a young woman's hair to introduce himself. "I'm Derek, from New York," he says. "I was a leftist. I was hateful. I would hate a person for injustice; I was aggressive in my heart. The Holy Spirit said, Derek, you're being a hypocrite. You're fighting the wrong fight."

He passes the microphone to a guy in ratty cutoffs and a T-shirt that says FIGHT THE LIE. "Listen, forty million people have been sent to an early grave," he says, referring to the number of abortions performed since *Roe v. Wade*. "That's not about left or right wing. It's for the good of humanity that we stand against this in Christ's love. Politics turns people against each other. Let's not talk about this in terms of politics." A smattering of hell yeah's concurs.

A bony, birdlike young woman swallowed by a baggy purple shirt receives the microphone in trembling fingers. "No movement has *ever* happened through voting. The civil rights movement happened through the people. Making abortions illegal won't stop people from having abortions. This is an issue of hearts and minds," she says, echoing the words of Martin Luther King, Jr.

From the back of the tent, a loud voice, taut with anger, calls her out: "Are you gonna cast your vote for someone who is actively making a war on the unborn?" The tent vibrates with applause.

Another male voice off-mic joins the fray. "I don't want my church to be a left-wing haven. I want them to speak out about what's wrong with the world!" Someone passes him a mic, suddenly amplifying his increasingly irate words. "*I want them to speak out about why my generation is being murdered!*"

I suddenly feel a body crouch next to me, tense with excitement. It's Erik Whittington, the head of Rock for Life, a wiry man in his mid-thirties, with olive skin, intense brown eyes, and a short crop of chestnut hair. He grins as he leans toward my ear, his voice electric. "You'll never believe this news," he whispers to me. "Sandra Day O'Connor just resigned. It's a good day. We'll see just how pro-life Bush is now."

An amassing tribe of twenty-somethings and teens in the hard-core uniform of jeans and black bandannas descend upon the tent as the session ends. Jeff Tragedy, a tall twenty-three-year-old in a dark beard and a black cap, takes the stage to announce the next lineup of seminars and shows. When he's not addressing thousands of music fans, Jeff books bands for Rock for Life shows and other antiabortion events from his home in Pennsylvania. The entire leadership and public face of Rock for Life is a deep-throated chorus of men who frequently repeat the litany "We do it for the women." This is no surprise, as the Disciple Generation carries the biblical directive of male headship through its churches and family structures, even its gynecological activism. With just a few exceptions—out of literally hundreds—every band that performs at these events is also a collection of men, each of which must agree to stand against abortion and contraception with "no exceptions, no compromises, and no apologies."

"A lot of us have had abortion affect us," Jeff begins after a brief welcome. "This isn't about politics. It's just about life. One out of three babies are aborted—but it's not just about the babies. It's what we do for the women. If we're a community, if we're one in Christ, we need to stand together." For Jeff, it's a deeply personal crusade. His mother chose to have him in spite of her doctor's stern advice to abort due to a mortal risk her pregnancy posed. Many people I meet at Rock for Life events are adopted, or were unplanned, or tell stories of their mother's difficult pregnancies. For them, pro-life activism reflects literally the fear of being themselves unborn. For others, it's a way to focus rage at the secular world.

Over coffee at a picnic table the next morning, Jeff admits that Rock for Life is essentially a sixties conceit, though radically opposed to sixties politics. "They did it first, sure, but we're doing it now. People find a home and a hope in music, a sense of community we all want to bond with," he tells me. "People who are over thirty-five, they'd rather take to pen and paper. We'd rather take to the streets. And I think we're more effective—just look at our crowds."

He's right. Beyond the bodies packed close to the stage, there are miles of tents and grubby vans housing tens of thousands of people who camp out at Cornerstone for five days of peace, love, music, and right-wing organizing. Most of them will stop by the Rock for Life literature and merchandise booth or music tent, where "activating" seminars run from nine to two. Afternoons and evenings see bands with names like Blood of the Martyr and the enormously popular Haste the Day interleave their deafening sets with antiabortionist declarations. Day and night within the Rock for Life tent, I hear many angry words of dissent against secular and pro-choice culture, but not a breath from a single person—"progressive" or otherwise—who isn't adamantly pro-life.

Such is the strange brew of the sixties counterrevolution. It was the Love Generation that produced the Jesus Movement and its lasting community, Jesus People USA. In 1984, fifteen years after 450,000 people descended upon a pasture in Sullivan County, New York, for the rock festival that would define a generation, JPUSA founded its own Christian Woodstock. Cornerstone was the first of dozens of summer rock festivals explicitly for Bible believers to spring up around the country. Here, the topography of land resembles Max Yasgur's alfalfa field where a youth movement famously tumbled into muddy anarchy to the sound of Jimi Hendrix's guitar. There's a gently sloping bowl perfect for a main stage, and plenty of room for the dozen other massive tents that will see nearly four hundred bands this week.

My tent lies on the bank of a small lake near the main stage. On the opposite bank a giant white cross greets me each exhausted morning—exhausted because earplugs are useless against the sound of crucifixion when *The Passion of the Christ* plays on the main stage screens after midnight; exhausted because I have learned that thousands of teenage boys, God-fearing or not, need no chemical catalyst to be utterly obnoxious at four o'clock in the morning. It just means they wake up without a hangover, ready to organize, open to the proclamations of the lead singers they worship alongside Jesus' message. If only Abbie Hoffman had had a sober crowd at Woodstock, his attempts to mobilize the cacophonous masses might have succeeded—though he likely would have had a lot less fun.

I would sacrifice a lamb for someone to lead me to a quiet and still place where I could see the stars each night unobscured by the dust stirred up in the mosh pits all around me. As it is, I blow off the Haste the Day show to escape into the air-conditioned pod of my car, drowning out the aural pandemonium by cranking up John Coltrane. I debate sleeping there, sealed off in my rented Ford Taurus, for the rest of the night. By the second day, it's easy to pick me out as the Jew at Cornerstone—I'm the only one sneezing in the infirmary trailer while a (gentile) doctor writes me a prescription for a steroid inhaler that will hopefully clear the dust from the dirt roads that has collected in my asthmatic lungs. Furthermore, this crowd has clearly taken seriously the sixties maxim *Never trust anyone over thirty*. I'm just six months into that scorned age bracket and for the first time in my life, I feel like the unwanted babysitter, the lone square unmesmerized by the thousands of sweaty naked torsos bearing tattoos of Jesus, making their way back to their single-sex tents at 3 A.M.

Sex, drugs, and rock 'n' roll—in particular, an overdose at the Anaheim Coliseum in 1987—were actually the genesis of Rock for Life. The group's founder, a mammoth bear of a man named Bryan Kemper, was born again after he spent a Bob Dylan and Grateful Dead show overdosing on a cocktail of crystal meth, acid, PCP, and mushrooms. While nurses strapped him to a hospital wall and forced charcoal water down his throat, a man appeared by his side to tell Bryan that God loved him. After his conversion, Bryan felt called by the Lord to sneak into abortion clinics, where he would stuff pro-life literature between the pages of magazines in the waiting room.

One day, from his waiting room vantage point, he saw a door flung open. Inside the room was a girl of about sixteen years stretched out on a gurney, her legs spread, her eyes filling with tears as a white-coated doctor reached down between her legs. Bryan ran home, ripped off his clothing, stood under the shower for a very long time, and sobbed for even longer, crying out to God. God, in response, he says, gave him the vision for Rock for Life: a national grassroots network that would rally young people against abortion through the subversive and transcendent power of music. In 1999, Rock for Life was born in Bryan's basement, where he ran the nascent organization with his roommate Erik Whittington.

Erik, now in his early thirties, "converted to pro-life," he says, before he became a Christian. The product of a teen pregnancy and an abusive home, Erik was chronically depressed; his sanctuary walls were the sound he could make with his guitar. Erik moved to Portland to play in bands and live with a girlfriend whose menstrual cycles were irregular even on birth control. Each time she said she thought she was pregnant, Erik found himself resolving that she have an abortion, even if he had to pay her to do it—nothing was going to interfere with his rock star dreams. One day, as he was driving through Portland, a "life chain"—thousands of people with picket signs protesting abortion—blocked his car. He tried to drive around the demonstration, but the protesters literally covered the block and wouldn't budge. Erik looked through his car window up at a sign that said, simply, ABORTION KILLS CHILDREN.

"My heart suddenly broke," he tells me. "I started crying, and I'm not a guy who cries. Ever. I knew what the sign said was true, and I couldn't believe that in my mind I had supported that." A virgin to political action, Erik felt a surge of new instinct, pulled over, and asked for a sign. "People were so caring. They were all smiling. I had never seen people like that," he says. An activist was born. It was years later, long after the pro-life movement in Portland pulled him into that city's emerging Christian counterculture, that he gave his heart to Christ. Driving down an Oregon highway, he saw a minion of Satan, he swears, "an actual monster," staring through him from the car next to his. In a panicked split second he accepted Jesus as his Savior, and never looked back.

Several years ago, Bryan and Erik moved Rock for Life from their Portland basement apartment to the Virginia offices of the American Life League, a Catholic organization. When the Supreme Court decided *Roe v. Wade* in 1973, abortion was a Catholic issue, not an Evangelical one. An influential Evangelical theologian named Francis Schaeffer thought the decision was an abomination, and was determined to incite others to believe as he did. He did this by developing a five-part film and companion book together with his son and C. Everett Koop, a then-beloved Evangelical who would later stoke the hatred of fellow believers when as Reagan's surgeon general he supported condom use to combat AIDS.

The book and accompanying film was called *Whatever Happened to the Human Race?* and featured graphic, wrenching abortion scenes. It was during a viewing of the last part of the film that Randall Terry, then a student in Bible college, began to sob hysterically and prayed that God use him to end abortion. An Evangelical movement was thus sown: a few years later he founded Operation Rescue, which defined pro-life activism into the nineties. From such small beginnings, today we have a nation of single-issue voters.

At Rock for Life, Bryan led by militant example, far more Randall Terry than Jesus Christ. He would protest at clinics with a bullhorn raised to his mouth, the ABORTION IS HOMICIDE T-shirt he designed stretched over his plentiful girth, his mohawk braced like a medieval flail. A couple of years ago he reversed his thinking, lost the mohawk, and quit Rock for Life, leaving American Life League to appoint his now former friend Erik to lead the organization. "Never, *never* will I batter a woman verbally anymore. I regret it horribly," Bryan tells me, his voice soft with remorse.

Bryan's shift in ideology and tactics—though not politics—threads through this movement. The concept of pacifism is rampant in this crowd that shudders at the notion of a preceding era of antiabortion activism, a time of bombing and murders, and the furious hatred embodied in Operation Rescue founder Randall Terry. The backlash against such activism has opened the arms of antiabortionists to a larger coffeehouse culture. These days, Bryan's image is of a bespectacled intellectual, heavy with philosophy and soft with sensitivity. At clinics now, Bryan opens dialogue with a sympathetic "How are *you* doing?" followed by an invitation to get a latte. Lately he has made plans to set up couches on-stage at rock events, have musicians play acoustic music, and invite people up to talk and have a good cry.

These events will be Bryan's contribution to next summer's festival circuit, sponsored by his new organization, Stand True—a kinder, gentler version of Rock for Life—which doubles the number of national antiabortion subculture networks, each employing a different strategy. The contrast can be felt between the groups he founded, both of which are organizing here at Cornerstone. In the vernacular of the crowd here, it can be understood as the difference between hard-core and emo. Each has its own draw within this culture, and each is running out of select T-shirts to hawk by the second day of the festival.

Selling T-shirts at the Stand True booth, behind a table laden with plastic fetuses, is a guy with teal hair wearing a dog collar. Most days here, I see him in a black shirt with an image of the American flag, only a white swastika replaces its fifty stars. Under the flag, his shirt says WHAT HAPPENS WHEN WE DON'T VOTE. At first I regard his shirt as a nice reminder of the importance of participatory democracy, a T-shirt I'd buy my dad, a rare slogan in this crowd where torsos proclaim a with-us-or-against-us devotion to the cross. I casually peruse the stacks of pamphlets at the booth, all filmed with the ubiquitous Cornerstone dust. One shouts, "ABORTION: THE HIDDEN HOLOCAUST." Beside it another is printed with the words "PERSONHOOD REDEFINED: DRED SCOTT, THE NAZI PARTY, ROE VS. WADE." Next to that stack is another depicting three images: an ownership deed for a slave, a swastika, and the round NOW "Keep Abortion Legal" icon, one that

I have held high over my head at protests since junior high.

My eyes wander back to the swastika on the T-shirt, and I realize suddenly: *I'm* what happens when *they* don't vote. To these dissidents professing Christ's love, I'm a Nazi in the abortion holocaust.

———

The Rock for Life RV is parked next to the tent. It's a fairly small, broken-down white camper, painted with the words STOP KILLING MY GENERATION! For nearly two months, the RV is a sweaty, claustrophobic home to Erik and his wife, Tina, their three small boys, and a rotating crop of volunteers. Erik invited me to live in the RV with them for the summer, touring the country. One look at the skinny bunk beds hammered together by raw two-by-fours and piled three high—if you're lucky enough not to have to share the mattress over the cab with two others—and I am breathlessly relieved I demurred.

One of the volunteers I would have been bunking with is Kortney Blythe, a tall redhead who is never seen without her army bag covered in antiabortion patches. Kortney is from a Christian family that is thrilled with her activism. She has just graduated from a small Christian college near Asheville, North Carolina, where her car's PRO-LIFE vanity plate was a big hit on campus. A few years ago she went to a North Carolina festival where Rock for Life was organizing, volunteered to help, and the next day drove ten hours to Creation Festival in Pennsylvania, where she slept onstage to guard the instruments. "My favorite things in the world are listening to pro-life hard-core bands and going to Washington,

DC," she announces. Like most of the volunteers, she seems pretty smart and hip, so I ask her if she's seen any good exhibitions at the Hirschorn Museum, or eaten at my favorite Ethiopian place in Adams Morgan. Kortney looks at me like I'm nuts. "I've never gone to a museum or eaten out in Washington, *duh*," she says. "I go to protest. Which is, like, the most fun thing in the *world*?"

Kortney sits in the shade of a tarp hung outside the RV with another volunteer, named Samantha Hammer, a twenty-year-old punk-rock pinup of bleached hair and black eyeliner. Kortney asks Sam for some Advil—she's been jamming black rubber ear stretchers into her formerly tiny pierced holes and the pain is killing her. Her goal is to stretch them five-eighths of an inch by the end of Cornerstone so she can wear ear bolts that show Jesus on the cross. Another goal—Kortney is very into announcing her goals—is to convince Sam to break up with her boyfriend. "He's not a Christian. It's that simple. You never should have dated him," Kortney says. "He only goes to church with you for the sake of your relationship." Plus, she adds, *she* just broke up with *her* boyfriend because he wouldn't support her life of organizing on the road.

Sam sits in a lawn chair under the tarp, picking at a bean burrito, dying to change the subject. At the merchandise tent, Sam just blew whatever was left of her cash for the trip on T-shirts and vintage clothing. She distracts Kortney with her new wares, holding up two fifties dresses and a seventies velour zip-up. Each garment is silk-screened with messages like LOCK YOUR COCK—a message of chastity profane enough to shock. Despite the heat, she's so excited about a new hoodie that she pulls it on over her shirt, striking Varga girl poses in her chair to show it off. The sweatshirt is printed with an anatomical drawing of a heart and the words THE BROKEN PARTS GET FIXED FIRST.

Sam is here to fulfill a profound personal calling. She was adopted as a baby—"sacrificed to love," as she puts it—by a mother who could have chosen to abort but didn't. As a kid, Sam had never really considered herself a survivor, as all Rock for Life members do by dint of their birth—a declaration engraved in the black rubber bracelets (this generation's armbands) they wear day and night. Sam always assumed she was pro-choice like the rest of her adopted family. But during her freshman year in high school she and a couple of friends went to a Rock for Life concert in Crystal City, Virginia, just to check out a hard-core band that was playing. The music was unmemorable—what changed Sam's life happened between sets. A screen rolled down over the dark stage, lit with graphic images of fetuses, both in the womb and aborted. In horror, Sam squeezed her friends' hands as tears flooded her cheeks, glowing red and pink in the light from the screen. "At that moment I came to the realization that my birth mother could have aborted me. That was me up there on the screen—my two possible paths. That had simply never occurred to me before," she tells me late one night when we sneak away from the music to chat.

High school was a steady descent into deep depression, drugs, and drinking. Sam would sneak vodka to school in a water bottle, and sometimes pass out so solidly at her classroom desk that she could not be woken. She didn't know whom she could talk to; she distrusted everyone. A Rock for Life volunteer named Mike had given Sam directions to the

Crystal City show, which she had saved as a memento. One desperate night she called Mike, along with his phone number, for help. She had met him only once, but she says she knew he was a moral person from his work for Rock for Life—to Sam, he represented agape. They talked all night.

"First I loved the music. Then I loved that they stood for something. They stood for love. They became my comfort zone," she tells me in a small voice, studying her black fingernails. After her call to Mike, Sam began wearing an ABORTION IS HOMICIDE T-shirt to school every day—to her mother's horror, a photograph of Sam in the shirt ended up in *Newsweek*—organizing Rock for Life shows, and passing out antiabortion literature. Through her new activism she developed a number of movement contacts, often people who lived in different states. When late at night she found herself spiraling into despair, Sam would go into pro-life chat rooms to look for people she had met but barely knew. It was to them, not to her family or friends, that she would unload her sadness and fear.

Depression has made Sam useful at clinic protests, she figures, because she can identify with pregnant women who feel hopeless and trapped. This movement has freed her from her own hopelessness, she tells me. Her unreligious parents understand that she needs a community outside her family, and a purpose outside her daily emotional survival, but they hate that it's this. Sam's birthday present this year from her family was permission to volunteer at Cornerstone, but it's hard won since they abhor her pro-life politics. Her father even gave her a few extra bucks to buy a Stand True sweatshirt she had coveted. The message it bears appears more personal on Sam than on the dozens of other people I've seen in mosh pits and at picnic tables in this same sweatshirt—SHE'S A CHILD, NOT A CHOICE.

Sam sparkles with compassion and intelligence, all street fashion and wit, her fierce spirit cut with stunning vulnerability—qualities I would have searched for in a best friend ten years ago, or would hope for in a daughter twenty years from now. She's the type of person who seems capable of leading a small battle if not a large war, if she can only get her demons locked safely away behind her. She'd make a formidable feminist, and maybe would have, if only a secular group, and not a network of religious right activists, had held the sort of events she would want to check out with friends; if only the phone numbers of women's rights organizations had begged to be called in times of crisis; if only leftists had offered the promise of love articulated within a genuine expression of youth culture.

This is a religious movement where for everyone the spiritual is personal and the personal is political. It is a crusade that wraps action in emotion, activism in salvation. People at Cornerstone tell me they are soldiers in a holy war, a culture war, a civil war for souls on American soil. They enlist for belonging. They enlist for love. Some convert to the pro-life movement before they accept Christ as their Savior, drawn into the movement by a personal connection like the one Sam made with Mike, or shaken by the arbitrariness of their birth or the suffering of their mother, or because they themselves are abortion "survivors" who regret their individual choice to terminate a pregnancy. Many, though, are just kids who need a community organized around an ethic that provides their lives with purpose.

Every morning around eight-thirty Erik creeps out of the RV in flip-flops, jeans, and whatever band T-shirt he was wearing the night before. He stumbles past the foldout tables that serve as overflow beds for several volunteers, past a dozen more bodies sleeping pressed together on the stage, and past the photo albums of aborted fetuses at the Rock for Life booth. At the coffee stand, Erik squints as the already hot sun hits his face; he pays for his double latte and carries the paper cup into the shade of a giant Jesus-topped totem pole.

Last night, long past midnight, a hard-core favorite called No Innocent Victim played a reunion show on the Underground Stage. Their T-shirts are rather ubiquitous on this scene—bold white letters screaming out from black cotton, I WOULD DIE TONIGHT FOR MY BELIEFS. Because of the late show, and a crowd that was adrenaline-wired long after the encore, Erik anticipates a low turnout for his 9 A.M. seminar on Terry Schiavo. Only a handful of participants attend—a couple of earnest girls in T-shirts, a middle-aged pastor from Nebraska, and some skinny, late-straggling boys. The conversation quickly launches into a heated rant of overlapping voices, each fueled with anger at the media and at Democrats. "Life has nothing to do with whether life is useful! That line of thinking is as good as murder!" one guy cries repeatedly as the seminar wraps up and a crowd of weary activists shuffles into the tent for the more popular ten o'clock seminar on "sidewalk counseling," led by a Rock for Life partner organization.

Saving Arrows is one of the few pro-life groups run by a woman. Its leader, twenty-four-year-old Melissa Powell—more blond dreadlocks and piercings—began protesting at abortion clinics with her family in fifth grade. Now she prays and protests at four different clinics, for eight hours a day, six days a week. "God has used me to save over forty children," she tells the group of teens and twenty-somethings sitting in a semicircle around her, in their dusty flip-flops and intentionally messy hair. "*I* didn't do that. *Jesus* did that."

Melissa closes her eyes, bows her head, and opens the session with a prayer. "Jesus," she says, "I pray that you bring those here who need to come." Her eyes snap open and dart straight to my face. "And I pray, Jesus, that you lead away those who don't need to come." I hold her stare for a moment and then glance down at my notebook. I know she knows: I'm deep behind enemy lines.

"We're going out there with compassion. We're out there to be Jesus to them," Melissa explains to the group, moving on from our momentary showdown. "And we don't think it's valid to kill for a modeling career or a car payment." She asks the group how many people know the hours of their nearest abortion clinic. Only a few hands shoot up. She smiles, knowing she's not preaching to the converted, to make literal a cliché—she's here today to expand the movement, to train a new crop of activists in the foundational work of her mission.

Here's Melissa's how-to primer for "interventions": Look

up your local clinic in the yellow pages, then call them up and say you want to schedule an appointment for an abortion. Choose a date a few weeks away and ask for the first and last possible of the day; now you know the clinic hours. Prepare some literature you can hand out, which informs mothers that their baby has a heartbeat after twenty-four days, exactly how abortion will kill that baby, that sort of thing. Set your "spiritual groundwork," meaning, before you go to a clinic pray about it. Make sure you're "spiritually covered"—ask someone to wake up that morning and just pray for you and the children you're trying to save. Then, you need to "work the land." "Go out there with other brothers and sisters in Christ and walk the land praying to lay a foundation," Melissa tells her pupils. "These women are looking for a sign. It moves them to see you pray for them, for them to know that God is looking out for them." At the clinic, worship God with all the volume you can muster. "People say they can hear us through the walls of the clinic," says Melissa, ushering forth a hum of impressed murmurs. "And that's the most effective thing."

Melissa's system is essentially the same as the model Randall Terry developed for Operation Rescue protests. He would divide activists into squadrons: some to counsel women, some to pray and sing, some to block the entrances to the clinic. The last of those efforts is now illegal, which really riles this crowd. The seminar continues with testimonies of clinic experiences, including Melissa's tales of locking herself inside various surgery rooms on "rescue missions." Then she demonstrates methods to get pamphlets through barbed wire. Finally she wraps up the seminar with a prayer for the salvation of the souls of "the mothers going into abortion clinics today," stabbing me with a final glare.

Erik's wife, Tina, appears early to lead the next seminar. She sneaks into the seat next to me, squeezes my hand, and smiles, for which I am grateful. Tina is solid, but cries easily; she is slight of voice, but unflinching in her ideology. Her eldest son, a four-year-old named Justice—so christened in the hopes that he will be the Supreme Court justice to overturn *Roe v. Wade*—climbs on my lap and leans over to tug on his mother's red bob; she apologizes unnecessarily and lifts him away in her sturdy arms. Tina has taken it upon herself to evangelize to me while cooking hot dogs in the RV. After she puts the kids down for their afternoon nap, she likes to read to me from a book that is a classic Christian subjugation canon, a guide to annihilating a woman's independence called *Lies Women Believe and the Truth That Sets Them Free* by Nancy Leigh DeMoss—"Lies like, 'I have my rights,' " Tina recites over the clamor and squirm of her restless boys.

Lies Women Believe would surely horrify Tina's mother, a former hippie and, for a spell, single parent after Tina's dad split. An atheist stepfather raised Tina when he wasn't relying on drugs to deaden his grief from a tour in Vietnam. Going to church with the same ferocity with which her parents abandoned it, Tina "rebelled by becoming the good girl," she tells me one afternoon while we're waiting out the midday heat in the RV. During high school in Portland, she used to go to parties and blast worship music; she evangelized to young men outside gay clubs. Though she "slipped" in her own personal life, Tina became transfixed by the concept of sexual sin. After Tina and Erik married, she committed her life full-time to making and raising babies, and to speaking to young people on college campuses and at festivals.

Here at Cornerstone, Tina lectures on many topics. One of her specialties is postabortion syndrome—how she believes abortion inevitably leads to depression, suicidal tendencies, drug abuse, and the need to master the experience through chronic aborted pregnancies. Another is birth control, which she addresses today, in a seminar that follows Melissa's training session. Tina begins by discussing the notion of a "contraceptive mentality," which, as she explains it, is based on the belief that the very notion of contraception is literally, *contra*-ception, or "against conception." Conception, Tina says, is God's provenance and our duty, never to be turned against. A young man (more dreadlocks, more piercings) asks Tina about Rock for Life's views on providing condoms to control the AIDS epidemic in Africa. She harpoons him with the same look I've seen her use to reprimand her sons. "Sin is sin," she says. "Why would we say murder is wrong, but here's the gun! It's the same thing when people hand out condoms in Africa. *Sin is sin*: There's only one answer: they should stop having sex." To Tina, as well as most members of Rock for Life, it's a simple concept: sexual "sin," contraception, abortion, all these things are tantamount to turning away from God.

Still aghast and outraged by his question, Tina scolds, "We think about ourselves. Did I finish college? Do I have health insurance? We don't go to God first. But God knows exactly how many children he will bless you with and how he will provide for them." She tears up and juts her chin forward, describing her two cesarean sections, knowing that three will damage her uterus, and that God may be calling her to have another. (Several months later she learns she is pregnant again, and Erik posts pictures of the fetus in utero on his blog.) "It all comes back to the idea that I'm a living sacrifice. If my sacrifice is that my uterus falls out, I'm willing to give that to the Lord. There is no greater living sacrifice to the Lord than to have children, no matter how." Here she gets positively medieval. "Satan has come to kill this mentality. And you should know that anything that hinders women in their God-given calling to be givers of life hastens Satan's work." A young woman sitting slightly outside the circle takes a deep breath, exhales, and defiantly slaps a Rock for Life sticker on her T-shirt. "EQUAL RIGHTS FOR PRE-BORN PEOPLE," it says. Pre-born women need not apply.

After the seminar, Tina and I huddle for a chat, during which she weeps about her self-hatred for marrying Erik with a sex-soiled body. When I ask Erik if Tina's lack of virginity bothers him, or if he feels tremendous guilt about tomcatting around the Portland rock scene before his conversion, he just shrugs and gives me a sly bad-boy smirk. While it's true that in most of the secular world—and certainly throughout the fundamentalist world—women's sexuality is demonized (while men's is praised), in Evangelical America this polarity is not just codified, it's ecstatically celebrated.

Today celibacy can be pitched, like all other aspects of Disciple Generation faith, as countercultural. High school students pledge their virginity nationwide at massive revivals called the Silver Ring Thing—funded by more than one million federal dollars—where the Lord is worshiped alongside the pristine hymen. At these events, teens ceremoniously don twelve-dollar silver rings on their left ring fingers in a pledge to maintain celibacy until marriage, as though they are wedding the Holy Ghost—it's like Acquire the Fire's *Semper Honorabilis* ceremony for an even more sex-fearing crowd. Guys participate in the Silver Ring Thing alongside their chaste would-be conquests, but if they break their oath, what's the price? For girls, since any form of birth control is out of the question, every opportunity for the pleasure of intercourse begs the penalty of unwanted pregnancy, which in this world is punishment indeed.

A pregnant Christian girl has three options. She can marry the father and live a life of subjugation like Tina, whose back aches from hoisting three children at a time, her patience threadbare from their needs and cries—no matter that she is a better organizer and speaker than Erik, and has a deeper heart for the work; he's the one in charge. Outside marriage, a girl can carry the baby to term and face ostracizing from her church community—which will damn her for her sin against God—and then give it up for adoption or raise it as a single mother without the support of her community. Otherwise, she can terminate her pregnancy and deem herself a murderer, carrying a burden of shame forever.

With these apparent and pathetic choices, I suppose it's no surprise women willingly participate in demonizing sex. It helps me understand why Melissa despises me and Tina is desperate to save me: I must look like a vision of Jezebel in this steaming heat, my tank top too tight to begin with and now shellacked to my breasts, my curly hair wild in the humidity, an actual book that isn't the Bible peeking out of my bag. I'm a modern picture of a godless Jewish harlot set loose on the heartland. Two volunteers have already asked me in the late, confessional hours of the night if I've had abortions, and lowered their eyebrows in scolding disbelief when I tell them the truth—I haven't—and then hate myself for betraying my sisters in secular enlightenment by not simply saying, *That's none of your business.* During seminars, Tina frequently tells her charges that "angry feminists" who want to preserve *Roe v. Wade*'s ruling are just women who have had abortions and need the law on their side to assuage their guilt. Each time she says this, despite their efforts to the contrary, volunteers slide their eyes toward me and then look quickly away. As a nonbeliever who supports the right to choose, I'm damaged goods by proxy.

The last day of Cornerstone, I hug Tina good-bye in a tight, lingering clench and walk to my car. In the dust on the passenger window, someone has used a finger to draw a large heart. Inside the heart another symbol is drawn: a swastika.

2

Come as You Are

In the shadow of majestic Mount Rainier—a sight that causes even me to murmur the words "God's kingdom"—lies the city that just over a decade ago defined a generation, the anticorporate, flannel-clad capital of grunge: Seattle. When Cameron Crowe wrote and directed his film *Singles*, about unmarried, unemployed, sinful, and seeking young adults, he set it here; the city was a metaphor for so-called Generation X. Just as Seattle was synonymous with that age, it is becoming a stronghold of the Disciple Generation through the leadership of a single massive church, one of the fastest growing nationwide, and by the time you read this, already the largest in the state.

At Mars Hill Church you'll find the very model of the new Evangelical movement: a bright candy coating of secular cool sweetening the bitter pill of addictive orthodoxy. This is no church where congregants shuffle in every Sunday, listen to the message, and then return to their extrachurch lives. At Mars Hill, faith is a *lifestyle* for its members. And this church is just the beginning of what thirty-five-year-old founding pastor Mark Driscoll has in mind. By the time I visit in 2005, Mark has already grown a twelve-person Bible study into a forty-thousand-square-foot church of six thousand members—that number is expected to hit ten thousand within a year or two. The church is just the beginning of his impact; he has recently expanded his reach through an organization that will spread his particular brand of fundamentalism into youth subcultures throughout the country.

It's Father's Day, and Mark is blessing babies. A stocky, square-headed figure in a black shirt and jeans, with a leather cord around his thick neck, Mark stands against a backdrop of a giant brushed steel cross and a phalanx of electric guitars, praying over the "lovely wives and godly husbands" lined up on the stage of his megachurch. In a husky voice, he reads from Ephesians about the importance of obedience, while dedicating children with names like Belladonna and Mac Vader—monikers that suggest these new parents' comfort in the worlds of pop culture or the occult, worlds previous generations of churchgoers feared as much as Lucifer himself. Mark prays for the continuous fertility of his congregation: "We are in a city with less children per capita than any city but San Francisco"—and we all know why that is—"and we consider it our personal mission to turn that around," he declares.

The way Mark sees it, the more babies his conservative Christian congregation can produce in this child-poor city, the more they can redirect local politics, public education, and the city's culture; it's the same idea many fundamentalist Palestinians have for gaining control of Israel. For those of you city-dwelling liberals who may believe that the religion debate raging in this country is as simple as *They have the right to believe whatever they want*, it's not that reductive. This sort of belief is no longer a private matter circumscribed within the church or the home. Seattle is one of the liberal capitals of the world, and within it lies a veritable city on a hill dedicated to repopulating the school system and the local government through a trifecta of indoctrinating, voting, and breeding.

Mars Hill is in a former warehouse in Seattle's hip Ballard neighborhood, where drive-through espresso joints outnumber churches about ten to one and a nearby billboard considers the theory MAYBE THE HOKEY POKEY IS WHAT IT'S ALL ABOUT. The church is a sprawling industrial space of corrugated steel, painted charcoal outside and muted taupe inside, where the walls are hung with canvases of a member's graffiti art, lit by Starbucks-style colored glass fixtures blown by a congregant—very decorator-does-urban-loft. Off the main lobby is a coffee bar and art gallery where members perch on black vinyl fifties-style stools, resting espressos atop their Bibles on tall bar tables. A cavernous lobby on the other side of the building functions as both the administrative entrance and the bookstore, lined with towering shelves of publications by Mark and Saint Augustine, as well as Christian perspectives on Tolkien and *The Sopranos*. Upstairs, cubicles and small offices house twenty- and thirty-somethings in plastic eyewear and jeans, running the church like hipsters helming the dot-coms of Seattle's yesteryear. Administrators here define themselves and their church as existing outside the slick American megachurch establishment, but in fact, these days, they *are* the establishment.

John Vaughn, the founder of the research organization Church Growth Today and perhaps the world's foremost expert on growing megachurches, says Mark's leadership in the Christian battle for cultural control depends on his great talent at converting secularists in their own vernacular. "Mark knows how to translate the Bible not from Hebrew into English, but from English into culture. This church is exploding because it is reaching unchurched people," he tells me, "and that is because it is both cultural and countercultural. The old church is like a museum, a fortress, not able to penetrate its culture or give voice to the culture." Mars Hill, says Vaughn, is the new church, connecting orthodoxy to politics to culture in a whole-life articulation of fundamentalism.

Celebrating twenty-first-century secular culture alongside nineteenth-century gender roles, Mark has developed a community that dwarfs any living experiment of the sixties. To say that Mars Hill is just a church is to say that Woodstock (or Cornerstone) was just a concert. Mars Hill wrests future converts searching for identity and purpose from the dominion of available sex and drugs that still make postgrunge Seattle a countercultural destination. Mark promises that his followers don't have to reprogram their iTunes catalog along with their beliefs—culture from outside the Christian fold isn't just tolerated here, it's cherished. Hipster culture is what sweetens the proverbial Kool-Aid, which parishioners here seem to gulp by the gallon. This is a land where housewives cradle babies in tattooed arms, where young men balance responsibilities as breadwinners in their families and lead guitarists in their local rock bands, and where biblical orthodoxy rules as strictly as in Hasidism or Opus Dei.

Following Mark's biblical reading of prescribed gender roles, women quit their jobs and try to have as many babies as possible, transforming themselves into thousands of Tina Whittingtons. Accountability and community is ballasted by intricately organized cells—gender-isolated support groups that form a social life as warm and tight as swaddling clothes, or weekly coed sermon studies and family dinner parties that provide further insulation against the secular world. Parents share child care, Realtors share clients, teachers share lesson plans, anime buffs share DVDs, and bands share songs.

The community Mars Hill members have built is truly utopian—this indeed is its great allure—but their code of living, delivered weekly by their disciplinarian leader, is a retrograde hell. Many women I meet at Mars Hill mourn the loss of their freedom, independence, education, and hope for a fulfilling future, but they tell me it's their duty as prescribed by the Book, by which they mean Mark's interpretation thereof; their liberty, they say, is a fair trade for community and salvation. Even in this progressive city that has offered leadership and innovation in everything from technology to rock to coffee for the past couple of decades, Mark has no competition for the souls he attracts like discarded metal shavings to a magnet.

"You're one of us," Mark told me when I first met him in January 1999, as if he were whispering a deep secret about myself that he knew and I didn't. "You'll get there," he said, offering me the prize of his encouragement. Back then, Mars Hill was an emerging community of a few hundred young Evangelicals. At the time, this seemed like a radical achievement—one significant enough for NPR to send me across the country to witness—a consortium of active seekers of meaning in the place that represented our much-heralded apathetic youth. The word "alternative" still held a fading flicker of sway in 1999, when former savior Kurt Cobain's body had been cold only a few years, thrift-shop clothing wasn't quite yet "vintage," and Jesus was someone worshiped by virgins and grandparents.

Within this culture, Mark launched a radio call-in show, which discussed Jesus in accessible slang and brought new members into his fold. He befriended some musicians who were writing loud music to worship God, and began to grow a church where members could watch Tarantino movies, drink beer, and live by strict biblical rule. To the congregants here, at Mark's direction, these behaviors constitute no paradox within Christianity; they say it is only generations of Christian culture that has scorned such acts, not the word of the Bible.

Back then, Mars Hill services took place at off-hours in a small borrowed church. The church leadership rented two huge Victorian houses near the university for this rising corps of godly men and women, who lived separated by gender. The night I first arrived in Seattle, the women baked vegetarian lasagna together, while the men chatted on a tattered couch under a shabby bay window as secular music hummed from a shared boom box. As in any cultish situation, a few roommates in those Victorian houses fell away, but most stayed, and married guys or gals from within the group houses, bought their own homes, rented basement apartments to new singles coming into the group, had kids, started up a children's ministry (and Bible studies, worship bands, and hiking clubs), and became the bedrock of this rapidly spreading community.

These days, Mark's reach within the media, which began with his small-time call-in show, has evolved into a column for the *Seattle Times;* his vision has become a phenomenon. Mark's ingenuity, leadership, and reach has surely branded this young pastor the Jonathan Edwards of his age. Jonathan Edwards—neither the senator nor the psychic—was the figurehead of the First Great Awakening, preaching from a pulpit in Northampton, Massachusetts. Edwards gave structure and support to young members of his generation, seeming to understand them like no elder before him. In his book *A Faithful Narrative of a Surprising Work of God*, Edwards characterized his era as a period of licentiousness, in which coed night "frolics" gained popularity as church membership waned and "family government" failed. In 1734, under Edwards's intimate direction, young people began to meet in small, personal groups outside church to practice what Edwards called "social religion," speaking about faith in their own language instead of the language of the church. One by one they began to be born again. This social religion—and attendant conversions—began to spread to youth in nearby towns, and then counties throughout the states. Throughout what had become a fragmented culture, Edwards wrote, the Awakening had set religious fire to "all sorts, sober and vicious, high and low, rich and poor," lit by the kindling of an ecstatic youth culture.

In every Awakening, religious revival travels via a younger generation that translates faith into its own idiom, guiding faith to the masses. Like Edwards, Mark has integrated faith and culture in our current Awakening to formidable ends. Brian McLaren, a hugely influential Evangelical pastor and writer who has tapped Mark to be a central force in his own organizing network, calls the movement Mark helms the post-moderns. "The spiritual resurgence that I see brewing is unconventional and even irreverent at times, largely developing outside the boundaries of our institutional religion," he writes in his book *A New Kind of Christian*. "If you were a missionary going to Spain, you'd have to learn to think and speak Spanish. If you are a missionary going to any educated culture on earth today, I think you need to learn to think and speak post-modern," the very language of Mars Hill.

Mark's attitude and barrel-chested form is reminiscent of a younger Henry Rollins, who used to grunt through sets of fifty push-ups and sit-ups before his shows with the band Black Flag. You can imagine Mark driving himself through preperformance workouts as well, and it's his tough-coach style of preaching that provides some of his appeal. He's the sort of charming, arrogant blowhard one loudly protests against, but still wants approval from; the cool senior you pretend you can't stand. In spite of myself, in our conversations I find myself seeking his attention, measuring my words for his maximum reaction, in spite of how domineering—and even sinister—his manner can be. To the many congregants here who had absent or otherwise negligent fathers, Mark doles out discipline with an ironic smile. It's not a shock to learn that Mark is the oldest child of a hardworking blue-collar Catholic family bent on survival and grit.

Likewise, his Jesus is no sandal-wearing pacifist. When Mark invokes his Lord, he describes an uncompromising disciplinarian who demands utter obedience from his followers in exchange for rescue from an eternity in hell. "Jesus pissed people off, so he got whacked," he tells me. "That's a guy with some edges. Marketing firms and spin doctors have been trying to round out those edges for centuries. Look at politicians, entertainment: Jesus has probably become the most marketable brand in the country. But here we just talk about him like a person, edges and all. And people know the difference; they know what's real."

The church's slogan articulates exactly what the Disciple Generation is seeking in Christianity today: *Truth, Meaning, Beauty, Community*. To Mars Hill members, these words function as a mission statement more than a sales tool, but to the uninitiated who see the slogan painted over the church entrance, it's a pitch or, more kindly, an invitation. Mark never views evangelism as a form of marketing. Because Mars Hill members frown on the traditional techniques of Bible thumping on the street corner, begging on televangelism programs, and threatening eternal hellfire on talk radio, they've had to consider missionary work of a different flavor, which they call "missional living." This is the notion that living well in strict accordance with the Bible, while reaping the benefits of a deeply supportive community, advertises the faith to the heathens by demonstration; it's how Mike at Rock for Life was able to convert Sam into a full-fledged pro-lifer. That demonstration is what is known as relational evangelism, or simply, the act of hanging out with an unbeliever until he or she is born again. "It's like Jesus chilling with prostitutes and tax collectors," hundreds of young Evangelicals have told me, defending what could be construed as blatant manipulation if their Savior hadn't done it first.

The way Mark sees it, America has been marketed to so constantly and shamelessly that it has produced a generation of jaded cynics desperate for what feels *real*. It is his edgy Jesus, he says, who best reaches a searching crowd. Likewise, he points out, this generation has grown up rootless and unparented, yearning for discipline within the very orthodoxy that Mark makes relatable and relevant. "They know there's more to life than waking up, eating what's in the fridge, watching what's on TV, and then going back to bed, than the rest of their porn-addicted, video-game-playing, loser friends. That's what I give them through the Bible: I say, let me give you some rules, not to be a jerk, but to help you out. And when was the last time that anyone in their busted-up family did that?" he tells me.

Since this community relies on Mark's concept that "manly men" should lead the church and their families, while women fulfill the role of the submissive "lovely helper," as decreed in Genesis, I am surprised to find myself looking forward to Mark's Father's Day sermon in the minimalist, cathedral-sized sanctuary this Sunday. But that's the rare draw of charisma and confidence, the mysterious alchemy of leadership. Mark's sermons are the bulk of each service, while many other megachurches rely on an hour of worship with arena rock lights and smoke machines. And unlike megachurches that attempt to attain relevance in their congregants' modern lives by offering PowerPoint-displayed sermons with immediately practical applications, Mark preaches every word of the Bible, straight through in order.

The foundational notion of the church is "culturally liberal and theologically conservative," a new balance of ideas that sums up the ethic of the entire Disciple Generation and separates it from previous incarnations of Christianity. It wants its MTV alongside an unconditionally loving and authoritarian God; it seeks the structure of a theological orthodoxy that requires strict discipline and adherence but requires no renunciation of hipster savvy. At Mars Hill the culture is always the best connector. While it would have been unthinkable in a church even ten years ago to invoke Snoop Dogg, the man who penned the memorable lyric "Now watch me slap ya ass with dicks, bitch," he plays a supporting role in today's sermon on Genesis, chapter 37. Mark conjures Joseph's famous coat by showing an image of Snoop in the coat he wore to play a pimp in *Starsky and Hutch*— "So the next time you read Genesis, think of Snoop," he chuckles.

Mark's sermon is a blend of comedy and philosophy that holds in his sway the thousands of people who attend one of four Sunday services. Pacing the stage like a stand-up pro, blending observational humor about parenting with ribald biblical storytelling, he peppers the sermon with references to his own children as midget demons and recalls his own past in stories about duct-taping and hog-tying his own siblings.

Between Bible verses about Joseph's many brothers he riffs about waiting in a supermarket checkout line behind a woman who said to him, "You sure got a lot of kids! I hope you've figured out what causes that."

"Yeah," he flipped back. "A blessed wife. I bet you don't have any kids."

The congregation hoots and hollers. "That shut her up," he mutters, closing out the bit to thunderous applause. Jesus, Mark figures, must have had the world's best timing to convince a pack of lowlifes he was God, and he strives toward that every week.

Mark's mood darkens as he discusses how Jacob shunned Joseph's brothers, and imagines their pain at not being anointed the favorite son. Pausing a studied beat, he looks out over his rapt charges and lowers his voice. "Some of you know what it's like. You were the one that wasn't loved. I can see it on your face and I'm sorry," he practically whispers—suddenly gentle after his booming performance of a moment before. "Some of you are still living life in reaction to your father. I'm here to tell you, you don't have to. There is a providential God who can fix you, and his name is Jesus. He's your only hope."

The sermon crescendoes into a prayer for his disciples, Mark's voice gradually swelling louder and more passionate, as a worship band tiptoes onto the stage behind him and slowly sneaks its guitars and drumbeats up under his words. His sermons reach an audience that extends far beyond his Seattle base—I have met people from Chicago to Denver to North Carolina who listen to his preaching every week via podcasting, and who have asked me the same sorts of questions about him I tend to get about actors or musicians I've interviewed. In Mark's voice, they find what their broken families, secular friends, or traditional churches have failed to give them: a home and a reciprocal commitment—if you swear by Mark's fundamentalist reading of the Word, his church will swear by you.

Such is the intense tribal mentality of Christian youth, made perhaps most literal by the tattoos that are ubiquitous in this church and throughout the Disciple Generation nationwide. If you ever want to feel startlingly uncool, forget rock clubs or art galleries—just find your nearest hipster church. Save for the pressed cuffs of the Young Republican crowd, tattoos are the assertion of the new Christian identity. They're a permanently raised fist, a black shirt, a green beret. Getting a tattoo is an authentically painful, not virtual, experience that is directly reminiscent of the nail-pierced hands and feet of Jesus on the cross, with the self-selected statement of a tribal marking and a deeper physical commitment than a wedding band. Every lip and eyebrow piercing is likewise a mini crucifixion. As Tom Beaudoin, a young theologian, expresses in his book *Virtual Faith*, "Though it has been more than a decade since my own piercing, the mark of indelible experience is ever with me, as proof that something *marked me*, *something happened*." Tattoos, he says, have even greater significance in our commercial age. "Tattooing is the only way we have control of 'branding' ourselves, instead of being name-branded to death," he writes.

Tattoos draw a line between the new generation of Christians and the old ones: in versus out, us versus them, hip versus square, radicals versus the system. Yet it's plainly a contradiction for this generation of tattooed Evangelicals to simultaneously swear their belief in the Bible's literal infallibility—every word is "inerrant" truth, they say—and to ignore the teachings of Leviticus 19:28, "You shall not make any cuttings in your flesh for the dead, nor tattoo any marks on you." The Christian Tattoo Association defends its practice by asserting that the Leviticus law was directed at pagan worshipers, not followers of Christ (it also reads the law to say, "Don't tattoo yourself, go to a professional"). Members of Mars Hill willingly accept biblical interpretation over literalism in discussing their skin art—but they scoff at it when gender equality is concerned, as lovely helpers strain their inked limbs to scrub floors and chase toddlers while their husbands pursue careers.

Meriesther Luce is a twenty-four-year-old congregant in a micro miniskirt and a shirt that says HARLEY DAVIDSON / DO IT IN THE DUST—all punk-rock black eyeliner and hair dye. Her weekly Bible study meets in a tattoo parlor on the other side of town. Meriesther was raised in a Christian family and was saved, she says, when she was four, but at every church she visited before Mars Hill, elders took one look at her tattoos and told her she was going to hell. "Whenever a church saw me coming, they'd instantly switch their message to preach salvation, and no one would sit in the same pew as me," she tells me, her voice shaking with an outcast's bruised emotion.

Her first tattoo, in deep black ink on the inside of her left wrist, says *Acts 20:24*, referring to the Bible verse "I consider my life worth nothing to me, if only I may complete the task the Lord Jesus has given me—the task of testifying to the gospel of God's grace." She tells me, her voice gathering strength in her outrage, "even with this tattoo, which helped me to stand up and say I'm a Christian, no one would accept me until I found Mars Hill. This is where I belong." So long as Meriesther commits to Mark's code that her life exists for her Lord, her church, a husband, and as many babies as she can birth, her tattoos and T-shirts will be embraced and celebrated in the language of progressive acceptance. Meriesther taps an unlit cigarette on her worn Bible and smiles sheepishly. "No one would let me be who I am until I found Pastor Mark."

The lobby of the church faces a parking lot; from the street the only entrance pedestrians and motorists can see is the entrance to what looks like a slightly seedy rock club, where over a darkened door, a small and worn marquee is painted with letters that say PARADOX. To truly speak postmodern, and to break new ground in missional living, what church wouldn't opt for its own secular rock club as its public face? Mars Hill's venue is named Paradox for the central conceit of Evangelicalism: *to be in the world but not of the world*. The club draws acts playing strictly secular music like the breakout indie-pop act Death Cab for Cutie; one night I show up to check out a set by ascending songwriter Damien Jurado. Through the genius of relational evangelism, souls sometimes enter the fold via connections forged at these gigs. To some Seattleites, the club is just a manipulative arm of the church—waiting in line for the Jurado show, I hear a guy yell out his car window, "You got Jesus playing tonight, assholes?"—but to many in this music-obsessed city it's just another choice venue for good touring and local acts.

Beyond the Paradox stage, as Christian bands grow in number and musical legitimacy, nonbelieving music fans find their way to Jesus through relationships built with Christians attending secular shows, or by attending Christian shows themselves. They go initially for the music, and then later for the message. Bubba Jennings, whose black plastic eyeglasses and spiky brown hair frame a sweet and pale face, is the pastor here who books bands for the Paradox, who himself came to Christ through a version of this roundabout rock 'n' roll route. Bubba was lifting weights at a gym when a guy approached him and told him he had heard he played the drums. He was forming a new band, he said, and he was looking for a drummer, but there was one condition: the band was going to perform only music that worshiped God. Bubba was just happy to play, and within a year, he was a Christian.

Bubba's wife, Shelly, in matching glasses and a jet-black bob, fronts one of the church's college-rock worship bands, and retired recently from her administrative duties at the church to have a baby. "I always thought I'd be married to a rocker," she confesses to me over margaritas one night. "Now look at me. I'm a pastor's wife. At least he's a rocker pastor," she says with a startling degree of sincerity. There's nothing ironic to Shelly, or most anyone else here, about this punk-rock piety.

Every one of the dozen pastors at Mars Hill seems to represent a different corner of Seattle's culture. None of them expected to lead a church; most never expected to even

attend one. Take James Harleman, a pastor in his early thirties with a ginger goatee and a steel cross around his neck,
who'd look equally at home depicted in hanging stained glass
in a Renaissance nave as he does in the Mars Hill coffee bar.
Before he was born again, James was an agnostic black-
trench-coat-wearing film geek whose hobby was to call up
friends and invite them to "come to the hypocrite show,"
where they would sit in the back pew of a church and snicker
derisively through services for fun.

That's what first brought James to Mars Hill, but Mark's
message and mentality hit him hard—in this church he could
watch all the violent animé he wanted and still find purpose,
meaning, and eternal salvation. Sensing that this was a pretty
good deal, once he could fully accept the whole resurrection
story, he returned the following week with very different intentions. Conversion followed soon after. James was friends
with an unbelieving, unmarried couple who were curious to
hear one of Mark's apocalyptic sermons on the book of Revelation, so they came to church just for sci-fi kicks; soon, they
were born again too. After Mark counseled them to split up
or immediately marry, they quickly wed; she quit her job and
was pregnant soon afterward. Such is the effect of missional
living when you're "a directionless slacker like we all were,"
James chuckles.

Over Thai food, which his rather meek wife obediently
ferries to the church, James references Kurt Vonnegut, East-
ern philosophy, and *Fight Club* with greater ease than he
quotes scripture. His role in missional living at Mars Hill is
to run a monthly evening called "Film and Theology," during which the sanctuary is transformed into a huge screening

room. James shows a film—movies like *Napoleon Dynamite* or *Hero*—and then leads a discussion about the biblical issues present in each narrative. He can't stand both the traditional church's condemnation of secular films and the passive way secular audiences consume movies. "Their notion of entertainment is to sit down and watch a movie to please themselves. I sit down to watch a movie to please *Him*. It's the difference between engagement and diversion." So agree the two-hundred-odd people who show up this evening to watch *The Incredibles*, a film more family-friendly than the usual fare but one James believes connects directly with Mark's current sermon themes of appropriate gender roles and family structure.

Like everything here, the evening opens with a prayer. Standing in front of a row of Goth parents, their faces powdered white, their hair dyed raven black, and their fidgety kids dressed in homemade superhero costumes, James bows his head and prays. *Father God, we thank you that we live in a time and place that we can watch something so amazing—a story with depth of character that has meaning to us. It's amazing that we take for granted the technology to be able to gather together for an experience like this that can teach us so much about our lives and your plans for us. I pray, Father God, that we engage this film and find within it character flaws, paths that are good choices and bad choices to enjoy with our minds on and not with them turned off.* I'm with him, God or not. But before the sanctuary darkens, James takes a moment to explain that the film demonstrates Christian messages through the father's similarity to biblical patriarchs and the mother's appropriate choices as a housewife. He tells the congregation about a scene the director was forced to cut from the final edit of the film, in which the mother is berated for shunning a career to stay at home with her kids. "That's a sad commentary of our cultural climate in which a woman should be liberated to do as she pleases, yet denigrated for choosing a traditional path," he says. "Our first instruction from God as relational beings is to seek oneness as husband and wife, and to subsequently have children." *Now that*, I think, *is a new interpretation of liberation: obedience to strict instruction.*

———

Jamie Munson is a fellow pastor of James's, whose road to Mars Hill was hardly transgressive. The year before I first visited Mars Hill, Jamie Munson was a self-described "sex, drugs, and rock 'n' roll pagan," drinking his way through his freshman year at a Montana college, when his older sister began to pray for him in her thirty-person Bible study group in Seattle. Within a year he was living in the Mars Hill men's house and en route to all-out discipleship—not through some lightning-bolt conversion, but as a result of his emerging role in the community.

Before he came to Seattle, Jamie used to lie awake in bed imagining himself fabulously rich and famous by dint of his easy leadership qualities and his business savvy. Those qualities quickly set him at the head of the Mars Hill men's house, before he was even certain he was a full-blooded believer. In Montana's backwater, Jamie had no outlet to make those dreams come true, but in this quickly developing community hungry for can-do charisma, Jamie could be an instant VIP, just as he fantasized—all he had to do was become a Christian. He began to head up Bible study, proposed to a woman living in the lovely-helper house, and decided to devote his acumen to the church rather than business.

These days, Jamie is the executive pastor of Mars Hill, where his office bookshelves are lined with economic textbooks and business self-help guides rather than volumes of theology. He is a baby-faced twenty-seven-year-old and father of three with a manner reminiscent of Alex P. Keaton, running the show here like a young Reaganite out of water. He has been responsible for strategically placing this church building at an intersection that sees a hundred thousand cars daily, selected for maximum visibility, and has recently purchased a new structure that will accommodate the quickly doubling membership next year. This year he was elected president of the local Chamber of Commerce, where he is the youngest member by thirty-odd years. "I never go to the Paradox shows," he tells me; "that's not my role here. My role is to love money and real estate and business, which Lord knows I do." He chuckles. "No one would be impressed with our résumés here. Just look at me—I'm a three-time college dropout. We were just called to this by what we see is wrong out there."

Jamie's view of evangelism varies from approved Mars Hill language: to him, it's business. "We're selling a product," he tells me without a trace of irony. "We're selling Jesus and the Bible. And what do you get for a life in Christ as a member at Mars Hill? You get community. You get authenticity. You get belonging. And what do you have to give up to get it?" Jamie asks rhetorically. The notion of renouncing nothing and receiving everything from Mars Hill is key to the message here. I sat in on New Member Day, when elders interviewed hundreds of new congregants who wanted to officially join the church. I listened to applicants fresh from introductory Bible class and eager to impress the gatekeepers, swoon all day over how cool it was to find a church that permitted violent movies, shattering rock, moderate drinking, and any sort of body art a young soul could endure. *I love how no one is going to ask me to change here*, they repeated robotically, ignoring the deeper obedience the church demands to a way of life that predates their grandparents' generation. Such is the allure of community and purpose in a world that offers little of either.

This allure cemented Ted Dietz to Mark Driscoll—that, and guarantee of salvation from eternal damnation. Ted was raised by a nonreligious mother; his father was at best absentee. In July 1992, when he was about twenty, bored, curious, and still living with his mom, Ted started listening to Christian radio in his room late at night or on his way to the mall where he worked in a dead-end job selling televisions. Every day he'd hear a preacher named Tony Evans bellow on about hell and sin, delivering warnings about coming judgment, depicting a tableau of fire and brimstone, frightening Ted to his very marrow.

Ted came home from a party one night, switched on his radio, listened to a few minutes of hellfire talk, and knelt beside his bed. For the first time in his life he prayed, fervently though cluelessly, a novice impelled by terror. "Fear is an entirely appropriate way to be born again," Ted tells me. "If we ever encountered God it would crush us. If you're in danger of being destroyed forever, that should strike fear in you. That's where all this starts for me."

Some friends in Seattle introduced Ted to Mark Driscoll a few years later. Ted and Mark discussed a new type of church—one that embraced the larger culture but was orthodox about biblical laws and values. Soon after, Mars Hill was inaugurated, the group houses were rented, and Ted moved in. Sarah, a counseling psychology student who had been raised Christian, claimed a room in the women's house. When I first met Ted, he had yet to take notice of the sturdy blonde. But when I returned to Seattle six years later, Ted had married Sarah and was supporting her with income earned as a real estate broker within the Mars Hill community.

Evangelical Christianity in America today is a grassroots movement grown up. New churches pioneered by young believers have set roots as formidable institutions, "the new establishment," John Vaughn from Church Growth Today tells me. What began as experimental living and spiritual exploration has cemented itself in the traditional American modes of commitment to marriages and mortgages. Now in his early thirties, Ted, a compact but burly man in a dark Amish-style beard, is a force behind this solidifying community, using his real estate license for ministry and moneymaking.

In the past couple of weeks, Ted has sold five houses within the church membership—"making our community more permanent," he says. The group houses were dismantled four years ago, when the landlord wanted to sell the rentals the community had long outgrown. Realtors like Ted replaced the group houses with title deeds, garages, and lawns that would quickly expand to form a new and intricate network across the city. Now there are no less than fifty neighborhood hubs that form centers for prayer, Bible study, and dinner parties throughout Seattle—local axes for Mars Hill's global reach. A megachurch of thousands threatens the deeply personal experience the church relies upon for intensive active membership. These cell groups keep the church intimate even on its mammoth scale.

Most houses are owned by young married couples who rent their basement apartments to unwed members of the congregation, whom the couples "mentor" until God delivers a spouse. Ted and Sarah recently reclaimed their own basement after they adopted two foster kids; adoption, Ted says, is another form his "missional living" takes. On one side of the city, the houses tend to belong to the Goths in the congregation, or the members of the Moped Army that buzzes around town in matching leather jackets, lining up their collection of Vespas outside the church for the late service every Sunday. Another side of town is home to most of the church pastors as well as a more mainstream set of congregants who wouldn't look out of place outside the city limits in their uniforms of standard-issue fleece and denim.

Ted and I chat with abandon as we cruise past twenty-four recent house sales in his pickup truck. Like many Mars Hill members, and most other young Christians I've met, he rides the ridge of a puzzling contradiction: Ted voted for Bush but talks like a quintessential Pacific Northwest progressive. "We're devaluing ourselves with consumerism," he warns, speeding through a red light. "The future is bleak for the United States if we don't free ourselves from corporate tyranny," Ted continues, now railing against Wal-Mart, sweatshop labor, the threat of globalism, and other standard leftist grievances. He sees mass liberation from America's fearsome consumerist and labor trends in the current religious "Reformation," as he calls it, but imagines this current trend to be a temporary one—not because he imagines secularists gaining ground, he says, but because the apocalypse is right around the corner.

Ted is extraordinarily well informed in matters of domestic politics and foreign policy, but he interprets all he learns through the book of Revelation. "I don't know if you know about this," he tells me, "but there's a new organization in Israel completing plans for the new temple. Jesus will come back and he'll take us—well, at least *us*," he says with a straight face, "and there will be an end to all things." He changes the topic abruptly to launch a monologue on Cheney's neoconservatism, until a Madonna song on the radio stimulates a hilariously funny discourse on his views of Kabbalah. Throughout my travels, I have had this experience many dozens of times: what feels like an enlightened and entertaining conversation with a wonderful new friend takes a sudden shocking dip into the realm of fanatic delusion, and then immediately jumps back to charming reality, leaving me internally bitch-slapped.

One June evening, I arrive at the Dietzes' small, pleasant home to meet the kids and join Ted and Sarah for dinner. Sarah is clearly exhausted from caring all day for two children, cleaning the house, setting the table, and preparing a nice meal complete with thoughtful touches like organic strawberries in the salad and fresh mint in the iced tea. As

Ted carries on about church affairs and lectures about the importance of children's obedience, Sarah serves the meal, cuts the children's food, minds their behavior and eating, and clears the table.

Every Wednesday the Dietzes' community group assembles in this living room, where vintage touches and contrasting paint colors suggest discipleship to Martha Stewart. Here they participate in Ted's Bible study and a discussion of Mark's most recent sermon; afterward Sarah serves dinner for twelve on an average week, twenty-five if the entire group shows up. Other nights their group gathers for less studious purposes but for no less spiritual ones; they commune in the kitchen—at least the women do—to cook dinner as music, laughter, and the constant din of small children fills the house and the backyard. The Dietzes visit other houses for her weekly Women and Theology class, where issues of submission and femininity are explored, or his men's group, founded to discuss subjects like pornography addiction and manliness. Like all Mars Hill local community groups, the Dietzes' clan was brought together not by preexisting relationships but by a mere zip code and a collective need for connection. "We were all hungry for relationship and for family," says Ted. This hunger provides members with all they need to develop bonds that become more significant, they say, than connections within their biological families or friendships they nurtured before joining the church.

During a community group evening, a couple of weeks before I visited for dinner, Ted was hanging out with the men in the backyard, while the women were inside cooking and watching the kids. Scrutinizing the dilapidated fence that had come with the house, Ted began talking about how he'd really like a new one, but wasn't sure how much the whole endeavor might cost. A few days later, the men in the group pulled up in front of the house with a pickup truck full of lumber and set about building a new fence on the spot. Now whenever the Dietzes look out their kitchen window, they see a proud and solid reminder of the strength of their community, and the unity of their faith in God.

Ted recounts this story sitting squarely in his big chair in the living room, his eyes set on mine over the rim of his coffee cup. I tell him the truth: I have wonderful friends who I have considered close as family for many years now, and I can't imagine any of them helping me lug the wood, much less building me a fence. He pauses and sets down his coffee cup in a motion that is about to put a definitive end to a delightful evening. "Listen," he says. "We have a really nice rapport. But we believe different things. And let's face it, because of that, you're never going to feel like family to me. So, what I'm saying is, this is as far as it goes."

Stung at first, upon reflection I can't blame him. I have nothing like his shared faith to connect me to other people, as much as I might yearn for a connection like the one the Dietzes experience daily. It's no wonder Ted and Sarah glow when they talk about their group with the same tones of veneration in which they join hands and say grace before dinner. It's not like the fence building was an aberration. After Sarah miscarried, the group prayed fairly constantly for her health, and for the gift of a new child. When they adopted their foster kids, two very sweet but exceptionally demanding and agitated small children with serious attachment issues and a history of abuse, the women in the community group were at the house constantly, cooking meals, looking after the kids, helping to paint bedrooms, sharing advice and prayer. "We could have never, and I mean never, made it through without them," says Sarah.

The Mars Hill community resembles the shared-land communes of the sixties far more than any traditional society of churchgoers. It's a little shocking to see this experimental model exploded into a megachurch that is rolling back the achievements of the sixties generation, its current emphasis on connection and meaning a tool to convert purpose-seeking postfeminists into self-described proud submission. Like every woman I've gotten to know at Mars Hill, Sarah talks about her appointed role within the church not in terms of subjugation but in the language of difference feminism. She tells me a sisterhood forms between women who celebrate their domestic roles and talents as offered from God, delivered unto their children, marriages, and community as part of his "perfect plan." It's a view that I never hear questioned.

At the end of the evening, when I go into the kitchen to help Sarah with the dishes, she confesses that she'd love to go back to school for her master's degree, but she just can't see finding the time. "I guess it's just not part of the plan," she says in a soft, distracted voice. It's hard to imagine that just a few years before, Sarah was a single girl tooling around the Seattle rock circuit in an old MG, spending her days studying Carol Gilligan. These days, Sarah's old copy of *In a Different Voice* gathers dust on the secular bookshelf (Penguin classics and psych textbooks) that faces off against the Christian bookshelf (Bibles and theology textbooks) in the living room.

It took Judy Abolafya, a young mother in her early thirties, much longer to accept submission as part of "God's perfect plan." As she sets out coffee cake on the kitchen table in her Seattle apartment, straining to be heard over her infant daughter's cries, Judy tells me without apology that she never wanted to have children. She shudders as her daughter wails, shaking her auburn ponytail and rolling her round blue eyes. "Listening to her like that just grates on me." She grimaces. In a high chair at the table, her toddler, Asher, glumly pokes at blocks of cheese with grubby fingers, periodically mashing them into a paste he rubs into his black Metallica T-shirt. "Let's face it. Asher is whiny and clingy and talks back. It's dull and tedious here—there are myriad things I don't enjoy about being at home, but it's a responsibility."

This life of homebound wifely submission is the opposite of what Judy thought she wanted, and the opposite of what she had. Her wall-to-wall carpeted apartment, with its refrigerator covered in alphabet magnets and a Baby Einstein tape chirping from her television set, hardly conjures rock 'n' roll bohemianism. Before she met her husband, Ari, Judy toured all over the world with bands like Bush and Candlebox, staying at four-star hotels, living life on her own terms. She made a great income heading up merchandising on tours, managed it well, enjoyed her freedom, and was confident and outspoken. Now she defines that behavior as prideful, even if she misses it. "Everything was great when my conversion happened. I was making money, I was about to take a trip to Mexico, I was totally in control of my life," she tells me. "My life is much harder, not easier, now that I'm a Christian," she says, clenching her teeth against Asher's droning whine. "We had originally planned not to have kids, but now we have to do our best to repopulate our city with Christians."

Her mother was sixteen and soon to be single when Judy was born. Twenty-one years later Judy herself had already married and divorced. She had found two things she loved more than her young husband: speed and cocaine, which she consumed in extreme quantities. Judy weighed seventy-eight pounds when she was rushed to the hospital one night and told by a nurse that she might have to lose a kidney. Remarkably, she pulled herself out of addiction without the help of rehab. (She once credited her recovery to her granite will; now she credits the Lord: "It's all him! It's all him!") Judy set her focus on a career in the music industry, and an English guitar tech who was soon to be her fiancé, though once again, not for long. Again she spiraled into addiction, and again she pulled herself through it. Years ticked by in bars and hotel suites, and eventually she met Ari, an audio technician in Seattle. He wasn't her type—too short, too quiet—but they fell in love, and everything, she says, was wonderful.

Some time after they moved in together, Ari seemed to change. He became emotionally removed and began spending his evenings in the bedroom with the door closed. Over time, Judy learned that Ari was reading the Bible, a fact that weirded her out since he was Jewish on his father's side and his mother's family was entirely areligous. When she confronted him about his secret Bible habit one evening, Ari confessed that he had been born again at age nineteen and had since fallen away from his faith. Living together, unmarried, in *sin*, he said, had reignited his faith. He was terrified they both were going to hell, and he wanted to start going to church. Judy was furious—she had no intention of shacking up with a Jesus freak; it had been hard enough for her to come to terms with the fact that he was "fairly broke" and "fairly retarded" when it came to financial planning. But Ari was a good guy, they had a good thing, and they had come this far already, so she agreed.

The first Sunday they went to church she swore she'd never return. They had spent the morning lined up with stay-at-home moms and their immaculate kids, all beaming like androids in their Sunday best—the literal opposite of the rocker life Judy had built for herself. Later that week, though, Ari heard about a church in a big warehouse space where the crowd was tattooed, the worship music was good indie rock, and the pastor was their age. At Mars Hill the next week, Judy was skeptical but felt at least culturally, if not religiously, at home in the congregation.

The second Sunday was the watershed. One of the church's worship bands was playing an electric version of "Amazing Grace" toward the end of the service, its loud and powerful sound filling the giant space. Suddenly Judy realized she was sobbing and couldn't stop. "I felt a brokenness inside," she describes, utterly matter-of-fact in her tone. It was a feeling of surrender, she tells me, "and I immediately knew, I'm never going to make it through life on my own." All day she found herself replaying the futility of different eras of her life, her years of self-doubt, her failed relationships, her period of intense addiction. Judy didn't say a word about her episode until that night, while Ari was strumming his guitar alone in their bedroom. She walked cautiously into the room, sat down on the bed next to him, and asked him to pray with her. That night she gave her heart to Jesus. "It wasn't like I was looking for a solution, or that my life was a problem in any way," she explains. In fact, the problems were just beginning.

Judy joined a weekly Bible study class at a Mars Hill pastor's home, where she first heard about the doctrine of wifely submission. The pastor's wife gave Judy a book to study called *The Fruit of Her Hands*, which can essentially be summed up in Ephesians 5:22: "Wives, submit to your own husbands as to the Lord." The author, Nancy Wilson, sees feminism as a cauldron of lies that have infected womankind, a view that joins her in lockstep with the author of Tina Whittington's cherished book *Lies Women Believe and the Truth That Sets Them Free*. "One can easily identify the weak-willed woman who has been led astray by this damnable teaching," writes Wilson. "Submitting to someone God has placed over you with loving authority is a relief, not a burden." When Judy stretched out on her couch one evening to read the first chapter of the book, she screamed and threw it across the room. "Why would I submit everything to someone who simply doesn't have the practical skills I do?" she still wonders. But she prayed to God and was led back to the Bible, to understand Wilson's perspective.

In the Bible, Judy found story after story about women

being willfully deceived, following their own desires, wreaking travesty in their relationships and homes. In these stories she saw signs of her own past, her mother's behavior, her friends' actions. "Just look at Eve," Judy says, "who was deceived even though she thought she was doing the right thing. You know what happened? Her husband didn't step in and tell her what to do. And now we're all screwed because of it." She began to submit to Ari about purchases and plans she wanted to make. "I always have to remember Ari loves me and loves the kids. The decisions he makes are for the betterment of us and our home, even when I disagree with him," she explains with a sigh.

Judy no longer reads secular books or speaks to her old friends, especially her former best friend, whose social life tended to revolve around the Seattle gay scene. A few months after I left Seattle, her family stopped talking to her—she suspects it's due to their "lack of understanding about my relationship with Christ," she tells me over e-mail. Judy is now a deacon at Mars Hill and is responsible for planning the weddings held there, which always include a biblical explanation of marriage and gender roles; each year Mars Hill averages about one hundred marriages between couples within the congregation, all of whom must agree with this doctrine. Between her marriage ministry, the women's Bible study she runs, her two small children, and taking care of her husband and her home, Judy says she doesn't have time for many relationships anyway, and when she starts to homeschool her kids soon, her time will be even tighter. "It's not what I ever imagined," she tells me, "or even what I ever wanted, but it's my duty now, and I have to learn to live with that."

The words of apostle Paul, and not Jesus, have set the terms of Judy's life. Paul told the Corinthians, "Women should be silent in the churches. For they are not permitted to speak, but should be subordinate." Furthermore, "If there is anything they desire to know, let them ask their husbands at home. For it is shameful for a woman to speak in church." Outside of church, the song remains the same: "I permit no woman to teach or to have authority over a man; she is to keep silent," he said in his letter to Timothy.

Paul was a murderer before he became a Christian and was known equally for his harsh diktats and his unmatchable spread of the gospel. Mars Hill is the name of the court in Athens where Paul attempted to convince the Greeks that Jesus was Lord. Instead of relying on his own language, and examples from his own faith, Paul addressed Athenians in Greek, speaking from their culture by quoting the poet Aratus and using their own explanation of Zeus's power to explain why Christ was the Son of God. This idiomatic approach has made Paul the hero of the Disciple Generation; I have heard his name invoked as much as Jesus'. Like Paul, missionaries who want to spread the Mars Hill doctrine grasp that they have to reach the unchurched within their own realm. They understand that in Orlando or Denver—or even the nearby Microsoft-rich suburbs—a different cultural vernacular exists than in Seattle's urban hipster sphere.

In the late nineties, a number of young people approached Mark Driscoll for advice about starting their own churches. His response was to establish a church planting network called Acts 29, which has been growing rapidly ever since. The book of Acts tells of the first Christians' evangelism in twenty-eight chapters, thus the idea behind Acts 29 is to continue their legacy. Through the network, new churches from San Diego to Albany have grown to follow Mark's strict orthodoxy and views. Acts 29 sponsored sixty new churches in the last year alone; 120 applications now wait in the queue for consideration.

While cultural specifics—media, music, dress, attitude, and so on—vary widely in the churches Acts 29 encourages nationwide, cultural politics do not. Most significantly, in founding the network, Mark has established a nationwide apparatus to push back women's rights through the "liberation theology" of submission. The online application for church planting is an extremist screening device to this effect. It begins with a lengthy doctrinal assertion that every word of the Bible is literal truth; the application plucks out the examples of creationism and male headship of home and church to clarify this doctrine. "We are not liberals," it says. "We are not egalitarian." In other words, disagreement will not be tolerated.

In the network, men who have not yet mastered a woman may not master a flock—only "godly husbands" may apply. Acts 29 is open only to the "extraordinarily manly man," says Mark's qualification guidelines. If an eager, married church planter passes an intensive online review, he is invited to a "boot camp" for training and interviews with his wife. At boot camps, Mark's gatekeepers consider whether a church planter conforms to the macho requirements that "to plant a church that honors God, a man must fight like a dependable soldier," "a man must train and compete with the precision of a skilled athlete," and "a man must sweat at his labor like a farmer." If an applicant completes the process, Acts 29 donates money and guidance to establish a church founded on Mark's principles, rooting his doctrine throughout cowboy culture, Nascar culture, mall culture, hip-hop culture, tech culture—anywhere heterosexual men reside.

Steve Tompkins, a former pastor from British Columbia turned techie at Starbucks headquarters, runs the network for Mark. In conversation, Steve reveals himself as tough, organized, and fiercely smart. His goal is to connect with church planters who will start by being sidewalk missionaries in their own communities before they begin to build the four walls of a church, "immersed in their own indigenous expression," as he puts it, "instead of the notion that there's a tattooed and pierced methodology." If a planter fails at organizing on the street and inspiring within his own cultural idiom, Steve says, the church will never connect like Mars Hill: "If you picked up Mars Hill and moved it even ten miles into the suburbs it would never work." People are looking for authenticity within their own culture, and anything that doesn't grow organically from that is bound to ring hollow. "I can smell the difference when I walk into a church," he says.

———

The opposite of Mars Hill, Steve says, is a giant church in a northwest suburb of Chicago called Willow Creek. Built entirely on market research, Willow Creek is the megachurch to end all megachurches. Ironically, when I ask John Vaughn to picture what Mars Hill will look like in a decade, Willow Creek is exactly the church he says he imagines.

Willow Creek founder Bill Hybels was a youth pastor

who hired a market research firm to go door-to-door to ask people why they weren't going to church, and what a church would have to look and feel like for them to attend. Their feedback became his mandate: in 1991 Hybels founded Willow Creek based on these surveys, and it has since become one of the largest churches in the country, with an average of twenty thousand people attending services weekly. The church looks more like a mall than a place of worship, with a waterfall cascading down the side of an escalator in the entry foyer, and two Starbucks-style coffee bars that flank an enormous food court. The main sanctuary seats thousands in a room devoid of any religious iconography. People told Hybels's researchers they felt that Sunday was a day separate from the rest of the week: they showed up at a building that didn't look like other buildings they would go to—like the office park, shopping center, or movie theater—and listened to people talk to them in a way they wouldn't hear people talk in those other places. Not anymore. "The food court is great. I can bring my friends here just like we'd go to the mall. What counts is reaching people where they're at," a young woman in a pink velour sweatsuit tells me between Frappuccino sips as we chat by the waterfall.

When I visit to watch more than five hundred people get baptized in the campus pond, a frat-boy pastor in cargo shorts and wraparound sunglasses plays the master of ceremonies. "Awesome. Amen," he says before each dunk. This is truly the conversion of the American mainstream. As anti-institutional as young Evangelicals purport to be, what I am watching—a mall boy baptizing other mall kids at a mall church down the road from, yes, a mall—can hardly be considered countercultural. As the counterculture swallows what lies around it, it becomes the dominant culture. According to the *Christian Science Monitor*, in 1970, only ten American churches counted more than two thousand members; these days, a church built on the principles of biblical orthodoxy exceeds that number every two days.

I think Ted Dietz puts it best, as we cruise the streets of Seattle in his truck. "You know the Ben Folds Five song 'Stan'?" he asks me. I nod. "It's just like he sings in that song, really. *Once you wanted revolution, now you're the institution.*"

78

3

Saved on the Half-Pipe

A dark November sky looms over the National Mall, exactly one year after voters renewed President Bush's lease on the mansion across the green. It's not the White House that tourists and locals are staring at today, but a giant half-pipe that has been erected on the grass. Soaring over the wall of the pipe, a skateboarder grabs the tail of his board in midair; silhouetted against the U.S. Capitol, his perfect human arc mimics the curve of the iconic dome behind him. A black T-shirt stretches over his lean torso, proclaiming in hot pink letters, HIS NAME IS JESUS AND HE SAVES PEOPLE FROM THEIR SINS.

Thousands crowd the bleachers that have been built here, watching a team of skaters dip and glide across this temporary stadium of rails and pipes. Signs all over the greater Washington area—deep into horse country in Virginia and the affluent suburbs of Maryland—have trumpeted this event for weeks. Nothing about these signs, or the demonstration before us, suggests the festival's designs on our souls, save for the T-shirt now blurring past me, angling for the next impressive trick. Indeed, the billboards overhead hawk not salvation but corporations like Amtrak, BB&T mortgages, and Interstate Batteries, none of which I know to be in service to any God but their stockholders.

But then come the decision cards: slips of paper that converts sign to signify their new commitment to Christ after being born again at any Evangelical revival, whether a Billy Graham stadium crusade or an event like this one. Volunteers begin to climb the bleachers, pressing these cards into the hands of the young audience, along with booklets entitled "Becoming a Child of God." If you were to listen closely to the lyrics of the hip-hop track booming from a DJ's booth above the half-pipe you could make out the words "I got a brother named Jesus / Last name Christ / And on the microphone I treat the girls right." The organizer of today's show, Oregon-based evangelist Luis Palau, has been here all week, leading a White House Bible study, taking meetings with senators and at the Pentagon, spreading the Word through the highest offices of government. Today, for the sake of effective evangelism, the message is more insidious than it had to be in conversation with members of our secular government—it's on a subtler tack, one that is all-importantly *cooler*.

The skater in the T-shirt is Josh Casper, who for eight years was a top-ranked pro skater, and the first ever to sail through the air on his board over twenty concrete steps. Back then, the notion of skater evangelism was still a relatively new concept—the provenance of a few church basements and suburban parking lots—and one that would have held no pull with this secular athlete who was inhabiting a teen fantasy. That was before Josh's father died, before his depression set in, before he took a longer recess from skating than his sponsors could abide. Josh found himself with a group of missionaries on a beach in Australia, beginning his Christian journey out of darkness; he came home to live with his mother, who brought him along to church, and the rest of the way to Christ.

This story, in part, is the testimony he delivers at today's event, during a break from his skating. "It's all about God. That's what I'm skating for. That's what I'm living for," he says meekly, clutching his skateboard, his eyes avoiding direct looks from the crowd that has gathered from all over the mid-Atlantic. Josh is living out what only the most starry-eyed and seemingly delusional skate pastors could have imagined a decade ago: shattering the air with his board just a hundred-odd feet from where the Constitution lies under protective glass, in an unabashed effort to convert all of us to a life in Christ.

In early 1998, on assignment again for NPR, I found myself following a familiar noise down the dank stairs of a church to its cavernous basement. The farther I descended, the more unmistakable the sound grew: the thwack of skateboard wheels hitting concrete. As I entered the room, the sight of scowling boys, their gangly bodies obscured by baggy jeans and sweatshirts, transported me back to high school parking lots far from the Evangelical community I was visiting in Portland, Oregon.

Suddenly the banging of boards stopped. The boys assembled in a circle, their dirty fingers holding on to a board or a friend's slumped shoulder, acne-ridden faces bowed in uncertain reverence. For several long minutes, they closed their eyes and listened to a portly redheaded kid mumble through his testimony. When he finished his story—a typical tale of Christ's love filling the heart left empty by his neglectful and divorced parents—my ears pricked, awaiting what I thought would be the inevitable cruel snicker from the cooler-looking kids at his side. Instead, gentle applause filled the silence. Then the skating started up again, the clatter of boards erasing the piety that had filled the room just minutes before.

I watched mesmerized, perplexed by a single question. *Why were such antiauthority archetypes widening their arms to God?* One thing was clear: these skate kids had something that their secular counterparts desired but would never dream of embracing in such a show of openness and vulnerability. This was what Christians meant when they talked about fellowship. But this was a Christianity I had never seen before, faith rebranded as a subculture for a country of angst-laden kids craving meaning and authenticity, a paradigm shift in the lives of disaffected American youth as formidable as the advent of the skateboard. Even though there were only a dozen boys in this room, they felt like the beginning of a movement.

Those boys represented a new generation, finding God in their own recalcitrant youth. A born-again skater named Paul Anderson cofounded Portland's Skatechurch—and indeed the entire Christian skater subculture—with a buddy he had skated with since their boyhood in San Luis Obispo. He was a competitive skater before he became a pastor, which gave him instant credibility with the kids he hoped to save. Anderson started gathering kids in skate parks, long before his Skatechurch building was dedicated in 1996, with an anti-establishment attitude at the heart of his ministry. Even the church's name grew organically from his outreach. "We never called it Skatechurch but the kids called it Skate-church," he told NPR's Lynn Neary and myself when we interviewed him for a segment; "what we did was just hang out with kids." Paul's slight frame, hoarse whisper of a voice, and languid manner belie his keystone role in the Disciple Generation, his crucial place in developing this movement rising from the wisdom of one guiding concept: "If Jesus was on the earth he'd have time for skateboarders."

Anderson's mission grew to include a phalanx of skate-pastors who began reaching out to the lost boys of their city, offering hope, connection, and community all mixed with *cool*, accurately diagnosing their flock's need for love and overtly providing it. This is how they got these kids to buy into religion, by delivering something larger than themselves, their troubles at home, and their adolescent pain, without asking any of them to change who they wanted to be. Their skills in the culture—namely their perfected nonchalance and ability to flip an ollie or land a 360—would lift these kids up to the version of themselves they daydream about in math class. The genuflection any kid will enact for a superior skater fosters immediate allegiance: worship the board, then worship the Lord. What I observed at Skate-church was an outstretching of arms made palatable by a snarl of authentic rebellion—a blend of youth culture and concern that hadn't existed in forty years.

I didn't know how my secular world could compete.

The tiny skater service in Portland has, in the years since I witnessed it, spawned a movement of at least three hundred skateboard ministries across the country. Even at the hopelessly behind-the-times International Christian Retail Show at Denver's convention center, Christian skaters built a giant skate park and ran demos all day under the heading "Twenty-Something Solutions." One of the best skaters there was a designer at a prominent Bible publisher, who was debuting his *Sk8 Bible* at a nearby booth. Thirty to fifty teams now tour the country to preach the gospel at skateboard demonstrations. In them, this Great Awakening has found a new grassroots movement of itinerant preachers.

America's Evangelical history began in earnest at the turn of the eighteenth century when a collection of young preachers relying on religious passion rather than theological training brought the gospel outside the meetinghouse and into homes, barns, and open fields, where both the curious and the converted would gather to hear them speak. Itinerant preaching was a social phenomenon in the colonies—a new form of mass communication spreading through charismatic personal contact. These preachers didn't speak in the vaunted vernacular of the established church; their words were the language of the common man, always translating the Word into the idiom of the day. The message they preached was not of ritual, tradition, or dogma; it was of simple personal salvation.

Their most iconic member was George Whitefield, "the Grand Itinerant" as he was known. Just as neat parallels present themselves between Mark Driscoll and Jonathan Edwards, anchoring Mars Hill in the history of American awakenings, so these skate pastors carry the mantle of Whitefield, an English evangelist who began preaching in the colonies at age twenty-three. He was like an early Elvis: singing hymns in a way no one had heard before and telling stories in colloquial language that horrified the old lights of the church. He lit the colonies on fire.

A century later, in the Second Great Awakening, itinerant preachers rode off into the frontier with a Bible and little else. They were the circuit riders, calling upon their mobility and determination to export their message of salvation to the most sinful corners of a quickly spreading nation. Living on the trail for months at a time, they relied on local folk to feed them, slept under the stars, asserted their authority by the mere fact of their survival, and adapted their message to what these fiercely anti-institutional pioneers would want to hear most. "It makes no difference how you get a man to God, provided you get him there," the eminent nineteenth-century evangelist Dwight Moody once said, and the circuit riders and their itinerant brethren of all forms agreed. This ethic rules the Disciple Generation as well. Pick your medium—what matters is the message.

These days, itinerants who are transforming American

Christianity are called "emergents" by the church establishment. The music and language may be different, but the method is the same, to take the church outside the church and the religion outside the religion. Just as this move was radical back in Whitefield's day, it's radical once more. This practice appalls some proponents of more traditional evangelism—what emergents often deride as "four-walls Christianity"—because they see old lights leaving their faith behind in the church sanctuary every Sunday. The old guard dismisses this movement as a deeply un-Christian trend—"the devil's work," I've been told many times—which threatens the traditional networks millions have labored to preserve.

But church Christianity is not what's transforming this generation. By extracting church from its establishment, the itinerants lure kids into this burgeoning movement. They are missionaries within their own country, working as hard for an up-tick in souls as they would in the heathen reaches of Africa or Asia. Despite its rhetoric of radicalism, Ted Dietz is right—Mars Hill *is* the establishment, even if it's a new establishment. For all of the kids who look to skateboarding to find their own system-snubbing tribe, this is religion rendered purely anti-institutional. Skate ministries are relational evangelism at its most deliberate, and often most effective.

When I was in high school, the radio hummed with the fake sounds of Milli Vanilli, MTV glowed in Poison's cloud of Aqua Net, and you could count the skater kids at any given high school on one or two hands, if that. "Indie" and "alternative" weren't yet corporate marketing terms; the notion that they could become Christian marketing terms was unthinkable. Skateboarding, in the eighties and nineties, was a response to slick, commercialized culture. To the kids skate ministries are trying reach, skateboarding represents easy authenticity with mass access: all you need is a board and you've got an identity, one that tells your peers you never mind the mainstream. It's an identity that still smacks of rebellious cool, though city skate parks have reduced the number of SKATEBOARDING IS NOT A CRIME bumper stickers, like the one I slapped on my three-ring binder sophomore year.

The sense of persecution by the mass culture that led to those stickers in the first place now feeds a Christian identity. Evangelicals effectively market the same delicious outsiderness that skateboarding once offered: be *in* the world, according to the biblical paradox, but not *of* the world. And like the Evangelical faith, in skateboarding you don't need to have a coach or a team, just a personal relationship with your Board and Savior. It's the romantic American ideal, really, and the one that the circuit riders lived by—*just me and my trusty steed.*

Seven years after my introduction to skater faith in that Portland basement, and a few months before the National Mall was to become a Christian skate park, I find myself in the heart of the emergent movement at New Horizon Church in Council Bluffs, Iowa. In the church function hall, seated around tables set with lace cloth and dusty vases of silk flowers, are a couple of dozen young guys with inked-up arms and beat-up sneakers, the skateboarders and musicians of the Extreme Tour. Since most of these guys don't worship in church, we're not here for religious purposes, only for housing and dinner. Some of them haven't seen their own beds for several months, sleeping instead on church floors (as I, with the help of two Benadryl, will tonight), spending their days in the van and their nights reaching out to youth. None of them are getting paid, getting signed, or getting sponsored. Unlike the high-budget machinations of the half-pipe missionaries on the National Mall, these are the direct descendants of the circuit riders, speeding across the American landscape with only what they can carry on their backs. They are the new itinerants evangelizing to some of the most depressed towns in the country—like this struggling corner of the Midwest—targeting kids like themselves to whom church has no appeal.

Even a bespectacled gray-haired church lady named Alice can't resist this group of would-be delinquents as she passes out baskets of muffins this evening. "I want to hear some hard-core music tonight," she titters. "Do any of you boys play hard-core music?" "We'll play anything you wanna hear, Alice," chuckles Ted Bruun, the giddy and overstuffed figure just shy of thirty who heads up the tour. Like any young man of considerable girth and wisdom, he seems much older than his years, yet so pure is the optimism Ted lends to every situation that it's sometimes hard not to imagine him an exuberant child heading up a very unlikely mission. Meet Ted anytime after noon and beneficence seems to expand his belly and push his fine blond hair from his scalp in fuzzy spikes; before noon, Ted resembles a deflated balloon animal, muttering, *Maybe Jesus wasn't a morning person either*. The parallels to his Lord run a little deeper than that—Ted has saved many of the guys traveling with the tour, collecting them as Jesus did his own apostles.

At the top of his form tonight, gearing up for an evening of outreach after dinner, Ted leads his disciples in a prayer over the meal and the work that is to be done. "Lord, I pray that tonight we would be deliberate, and I pray that when they look at us tonight, they would see your love. That would be cool, Lord," he says, bowing his head. After dinner, tour members will head strategically for wherever young people hang out—in this case the skate park, the mall, and the bowling alley—for "hype night," an evening of chatting up local youth before tomorrow's skate demo and band showcase. Ted's idea is that the only people you can reach are the people you connect with, so he wants tomorrow's crowd not to feel that they're attending a random performance, but that they're *with* the band, or auditioning for the skate team. This is relational evangelism at its most intentional. It's a tough task to pull off in two nights before the tour vans roll on to the next destination.

As the guys tuck into Alice's excellent casserole, Ted remains standing to lecture the gang on the specific woes facing Council Bluffs, all of which he's learned from locals since he pulled into town this afternoon. It's a pretty dreary place, so bad that residents believe Native Americans placed a curse on the area after a brutal massacre during the pioneer days. There's a meth epidemic here, and rampant sexual and physical abuse; depression is more common than not, and almost never treated. The new casinos—recently built to jump-start the town's desperate economy—have generated huge gambling problems and debt, the latter easily traced to the massive proliferation of hawk shops along the highway. "Even if

89

any of these kids don't have these problems themselves, they probably live with one. So be sensitive. And know that this isn't a show, it's not about skating, it's not about music. It's about the answer we find in Christ. It's not about politics. It's about the love and peace we've found. They need it here, too, so let's help them find it," he says. "And let's call on God to help us be real before them. They know the difference."

Fifteen years ago, Ted was a high school outcast in rural Idaho, the kid alone in the lunchroom, overweight, shy, and awkward. The summer before his senior year, goofing around in the wilderness, he tumbled seventy-two feet off a cliff onto his head. His skull should have shattered and his neck should have broken, but somehow he was relatively unharmed by the fall. In intensive care later that day, a neurologist stood by his bedside, shaking his head at Ted in wonder. "I don't believe in God," he said, "but I honestly can't explain any other way you're sitting here." In that moment Ted told himself that if his life was important enough to God to save, then God could have it.

After high school, Ted overcame his shyness and became a youth pastor at a church in Twin Falls, Idaho, a town of thirty thousand where the murder rate was soaring. Kids looking for belonging and discipline were finding both not in church but in gang membership, so Ted would go out to meet the gangs and tell them he wanted to start throwing parties at the church. Knowing that the word "church" was up there with "cops" on the list of greatest turnoffs, he told them, "Why don't you come and be my expert? Tell me what you want to see at this party, and we'll throw it together."

Every week attendance would double, until Ted had created a veritable brand-new youth culture in Twin Falls.

But church members despised him for bringing these kids into their midst. During one service, Ted reported to the congregation about a major success the night before, the sort of achievement youth workers dream of: a mass of kids had flushed their entire drug stash down the toilets in the church bathroom. Instead of applauding, a parishioner shouted, "Do you know what that can do to our plumbing?" and walked out, a line of grumbling dissenters forming behind him.

Half the church left because of Ted's new congregants. They said they were sick of finding a new pew to sit in after a tattooed kid joined theirs, and sick of wondering if these new converts might bring guns into the sanctuary, or when a fight would break out—though none ever did. Ted began to feel that church mentality was no different than gang mentality—an exclusive group with a dress code and a set of rules to live by, where no deviation from the institution would be tolerated. And so several years ago Ted left the church, too. He couldn't stop thinking about how God sent out the apostles to spread the Word, and told them not to take a purse, not to take an extra pair of shoes, just to take his message to the people who needed it most. Ted bought a van on eBay for $700—about what Ken Kesey paid for his Magic Bus, I believe—assembled a band of disciples wielding skateboards and guitars, and the Extreme Tour was born: a sixties-style communal caravan on an Evangelical mission.

While these guys are not about to lead me to Christ, in their loving presence I repeatedly feel warmth in my heart, if not a tug upon it. Were I someone who felt hopeless and lonely, with only the solitary comfort of my skateboard or my headphones, seeking certainty in a maddening world, I can imagine finding a home in this gang. They offer all the prankish irreverence of MTV's *Jackass* crew, but cut with a depth and earnestness that this generation most often fears like a contagious disease. Don't get me wrong: all these guys are straight-up Jesus freaks who live and breathe a holy trinity of music, skating, and, most crucially, the calling to convert. They want to save my soul as much as anyone else in the Christian world—perhaps even more, considering the lifestyle they opt to lead to maximize the effectiveness of their evangelism.

Down the highway from the new casinos, across the railroad tracks, and beside an abandoned utilities building lies the cement ramps and half-pipes of the municipal skateboard park. Under a crystalline July sky, a crowd of eleven-to-fourteen-year-olds watch in awe as the older, cooler, confident Extreme Tour skaters stride through the park gates like out-of-town cowboys in an old Western. The team is a tight-knit crew of Latino and black skaters who've been tearing up skate parks and church hallways all over the country for months, but they go back even further.

Angelo Gonzales, a hulking Mexican-American in hipster-frame eyeglasses, built a skate ministry at a Dallas church that grew from two to forty within its first month. The guys Angelo skates with today are mainly souls he saved in Dallas through the lure of a decent skate park—teens who would take two buses and a train to skate his excellent rails and endure a mere fifteen minutes of preaching a session. Angelo's church experience reflected Ted's; he, too, realized that this generation could be reached only outside a sanctuary. Ted picked up Angelo and some of his skaters at a Dallas stop a few years ago and christened him the Extreme Tour skate pastor as well as one of its headlining hip-hop acts.

As soon as the team swaggers into the park, the bravest young punk in the vicinity—all bleached hair and torn denim—guardedly saunters up to Angelo, cocks his head, and demands, "Where'd you get that board at?" For three hours, as dusk falls over Council Bluffs, the Extreme Tour skates for Jesus, but never mentions his name. The crowd quickly grows—word travels fast when a skate team comes to a town where *no one* comes—as local kids reveal how impressed they are by how hard they try to act and sound unimpressed. Mingling together at the top of the half-pipe, the locals and tour guys show one another their scars, chat about the local board shop, and periodically drop into a trick off the edge of the rounded wall, their lean figures stark against the sky for a moment, gliding through the air like angels in loose T-shirts. Occasionally Angelo says to an awestruck kid, "Check it out. We're doing a skate demo tomorrow, and we're holding a competition to see who will be touring with our team next year," and within minutes, new cells of possible converts cluster to murmur about the next day's event.

"You going to the competition tomorrow?"

"What competition?"

"You didn't hear about it?"

Once darkness falls, the skaters and bands head over the river into Omaha's old market neighborhood, where renovated lofts line cobblestone streets near the waterfront. Each guy holds a sheaf of flyers for the next day's show—none mention the event's larger purpose—attempting to meet local unbelievers in their own way. The band from New Jersey flirts with girls in tube tops, grinning like they're in a boy band video. Ted and his staff buys a case of Diet Cokes and hands them out to homeless kids in a park, offering to pick them up in the van and bring them to Rebels, the club where the show will take place. And Freddie Fisher, a musician of indiscriminate age—young enough to hang, old enough to seem like he's been to hell and back—just pulls his cap down over his greasy hair until the bill obscures his murky brown eyes. In his feline saunter, Freddie prowls the streets, the flyers in his hand coated with a layer of his elusive cool.

A kid with spiked hair, jittery on something—Freddie guesses meth, and he'd know—walks by with his hand raised, demanding a high five, and says his name is Aryan. Freddie introduces himself, blasé as can be, and hands the kid a flyer.

"So, man, you like write songs about girls and all that?" Aryan asks Freddie.

Freddie snickers, knowing he writes songs only about God. "No, man. I don't write songs about girls at all."

If Johnny Cash were still alive and looking for songwriting material, he'd hit pay dirt in the narrative of Freddie Fisher. Freddie's mom split when he was a little kid; he spent his childhood riding around in his dad's cab in Birmingham, getting high off his father's pot fumes while listening to his apocalyptic Christian tapes. The first time he ever took a hit himself he was a teen in the back of a band's van. Freddie thought he had a fairly innocuous joint between his fingers; turns out it was heroin. He picked up the needle soon afterward.

A stint in jail for writing forged checks didn't get Freddie off smack, but after a decade of addiction and related antics in which he developed a habit of quitting bands onstage in the middle of career-making shows, he freed himself, only to spiral again. The catalyst this time was his mother, with whom he had reconnected, who stole money from him to buy the methamphetamines that delivered her a fatal overdose. Freddie joined the Extreme Tour not so much to evangelize as to be ministered to himself, to be kept in line by guys walking a straighter path alongside him. Still, it is Freddie who often connects most with the people Ted and his crew are trying to reach. His laid-back star quality and drawl-laced mumble radiate the authenticity for which this generation clamors.

Aryan is visibly thrilled when Freddie asks if he wants to get a cup of coffee with him and a fellow Extreme Tour member, a goateed and shaved-headed former Mennonite named Jerimae Yoder, whose cerebral and soulful presence has lifted him up as the worship leader and spiritual guardian of the group. The guys command a ring of couches in a nearby café. Aryan leans forward, gripped by every word of the conversation about the institutional problems of the church.

"Gandhi said if it wasn't for Christians he'd be a Christian," says Jerimae. "It's not about religion. Religion is the problem. There's a whole new culture and whole new church emerging and it's not about a building; it's about people talking in coffeehouses just like we are now. It's about people in skate parks. It's about a new music movement. It's about something real."

"Wow, man. That sounds awesome," says Aryan, eyes wide, practically tumbling off the upholstery. "I'm really digging your insight."

"You have no idea, man," says Freddie. "You should roll with us and see."

The next afternoon, Ted pulls the van up in front of Rebels nightclub, a white box of peeling paint where this latter-day happening will be held. Rebels is innocuous outside, a low concrete rectangle in a wasteland of warehouses, but inside its single slit of a window its biker bar roots expose themselves in the black-painted walls, pool tables, and posters for leather-clad bands. The owners used to work here—he was the bouncer, she was the bartender—until they both were thrown in jail and transformed in their respective cells from hell's angels to heaven's shills. When they got out, they bought their former den of sin to convert it into a Christian haven.

Aryan is inside hanging out with Freddie, as are the tube-top girls who flirted with the boy band the night before; the skaters have multiplied and are trying to one-up each other on the makeshift skate park the team has set up on the street outside. But for Ted, the most important component is climbing out of the van: the crowd of homeless kids he befriended the night before. "When does anyone ever do anything for them?" he asks the crew in their preshow meeting. "Tonight we need to put on a great party just for them. If they can see what we can do for them through God's love, they'll begin to understand what God can do for them."

Outside, the skate "competition" continues in an utterly secular fashion, as Ted takes the stage inside. No mention of God will be made for quite some time, and none in earnest for hours until after the ramps are packed up. The bands with the least overtly Christian vibe perform first, "Christian" just because their lyrics don't glorify sex or violence; the bands that write music explicitly about Christ hit the stage long after everyone is comfortable. All along, Ted tends the crowd like the world's best—and least inhibited—bar mitzvah DJ. He raises the roof during hip-hop sets, and sits on the stage and sings along during acoustic sets. The most sneering and skeptical kids cleave to him and play along, guffawing at his jokes, getting down with his jiggling and ridiculous dance moves, unable to resist his utter warmth. The bands respond in turn, playing vigorous sets to this small crowd that has no cash to blow on their albums or T-shirts. By the time the music becomes more Christ-centered, hearts are open, bodies are relaxed, the postmodern be-in is in full swing.

As Freddie unlatches his guitar case onstage, Ted takes the mike and begins to weave the message into the evening. "I know a lot of people who tell you about God are real jackasses, and I'm sorry about that," he says quietly to the crowd huddled around him. "They've been real jackasses to me, too. But we're not about that. We're about sharing his love.

There ain't no church that told us to put this party on for you tonight. We put this party on for you so you can feel our love and God's love, and think back on tonight and remember that feeling, that love, whenever you need it." Then he introduces Freddie, who has taken a seat on a stool and pulled his cap down low over his eyes. "The cool thing about Freddie is he got kicked out of church, too." Freddie plays an acoustic set about addiction, overdose, and desperation, and finally about God's love. The chorus of his last song, "Hallelujah" repeated over and over, is a beatific coffeehouse liturgy that wets eyes through the room. Angelo's hip-hop act follows, his voice booming a cappella after the sound system fails. A rap about a suicide attempt elicits sobs from one homeless girl, who joins Angelo in the back of the club after his performance, where she lays her head on his massive chest and cries some more.

Toward the end of the evening, Ted stands onstage and prays for a long time to end all the addiction and heartache in the room. He asks the crowd if anyone has something in particular they need prayer for, and most of the hands below the stage—scarred and dirty from homelessness or skateboarding—rise immediately. After personal prayer the local kids disperse, and Jerimae takes the stage to lead worship for the Extreme Tour skaters and musicians. He closes his eyes and says a prayer I know is meant for me. "Jesus," he prays, "if there's anyone here who you could look in the eye and say, *I don't know you*, I pray you can change their hearts."

I am touched, for once, and less creeped out by his words than I would have anticipated. I may not yet want to take

Jesus Christ into my heart, but Jerimae, Ted, Freddie, and the rest of these guys have attached themselves somewhere deep inside me. There they will remain, departing Council Bluffs for their next stop, their lingering presence still slowly melting away my icy skepticism long after their guitar riffs and kick-flips are vague and shadowy memories.

The Extreme Tour holds no altar call asking people who want to give their heart to Christ to come forward to sign a decision card. Most Evangelical groups, though they deny it, measure their effectiveness by simply counting the numbers of souls saved. Soul counting is the sort of thing Ted associates with the institution of the church, an attitude that communicates, *You're in the club or you're out.* Ted's mission is so antiestablishment that he has turned down offers to market the tour to 275,000 churches nationally, offers that would bring in loads of cash and exposure. Since that's not what Jesus or his apostles did, it's not what Ted plans to do. "The day the crew sleeps in hotel rooms instead of on church floors, or eats out at restaurants instead of church kitchens, is the day the tour will lose its heart," Ted tells me. "The last thing we should be doing is living like Hollywood people," he says with a shy grin.

Evangelicalism's latest poster boy is the embodiment of "Hollywood people": actor Stephen Baldwin, who, on the National Mall that November afternoon, lumbered onto the half-pipe in giant aviator sunglasses to testify to his recent "gnarly" rebirth in Christ. Baldwin is the sort of B-lister who answers his cell phone to talk to his agent in the middle of outreach events. He has had his faith profiled in *GQ;* skaters who travel with him call him "Stephen Baldwin," as though he is inseparable from his boldface name. "Every few years some new celebrity anoints themselves the new face of Christianity," one Evangelical culture maker told me, provided I wouldn't share his name. "They draw out huge amounts of attention and completely fail to truly understand Christ's message. For a few years it was Kirk Cameron," from the eighties sitcom *Growing Pains*, who produced and starred in the big-screen version of the hugely popular book *Left Behind*. "Now the biggest joke—not that you'd know it from his numbers—is Stephen Baldwin." You wouldn't know it from his political profile either. President Bush recently appointed Baldwin an advisor on cultural issues relating to youth, and Baldwin was selected to speak at the Republican National Convention, where he announced proudly from the podium, "I'm here because of my faith."

A couple of years ago a newly faithful Stephen Baldwin signed up with the Luis Palau Association, the Evangelical juggernaut that held the Washington revival and that Skate-church's Paul Anderson now calls home. Baldwin offered to direct a video of top-ranked skaters flipping tricks and talking about their lives in Christ. *Livin It* was the DVD that resulted, an infomercial for Jesus directed at heathen teens. It's a typical skate video: all low angles under leaping boards, quick intercuts, grainy stock, a sound track of hip-hop and California surf punk, and behind-the-scenes antics of skaters pelting one another with McDonald's fries between dips into the half-pipe. Following the gospel of "sneaky deep," Christianity isn't mentioned for the bulk of the video, save for a brief moment when Baldwin looms into the lens and lauds one muttonchopped skater as his "gangsta for Jesus."

Only after the skateboarders have wowed the viewer with their athletic prowess and hip haircuts is the purpose of the video revealed. Then, in an insidious seduction of the viewer—who we can imagine hunched perilously alone in his messy, sweat-smelling bedroom, acne-pitted cheeks lit by the glow of his television screen—Christian music fades up under a montage of soulful camaraderie. Skaters stand together in prayer circles, arms wrapped tight around one another's shoulders, exchanging meaningful smiles. It's the very picture of belonging, a visual distillation of what it feels like to be *in*, to experience all that the viewer might crave. Then the music dips under a voice-over of skaters' testimonies, voices cut together phrase after phrase, intoning "true purpose" and "eternal comfort." The video ends with an invitation to watch Paul Anderson's message about God, which is a brief primer on the basic promises of the New Testament. "When you meet Jesus you become a new person," he pitches. At the end of the lesson, Paul looks into the camera and invites the viewer to bow his head and say the sinner's prayer, the words one utters upon devoting one's life to Jesus. "If you meant it and prayed that, you're one of our brothers," Paul says. "You're a child of God, and you're stoked, man."

Livin It was expected to sell 20,000 copies in four years—it sold 150,000 in fifteen months. Within its first year of release, fifteen thousand people sent e-mails to tell Baldwin they converted because of the video. Riding this success, Stephen Baldwin and the Palau Association launched a Livin

It skateboarding tour, which drew an audience of more than a million in its first year, selling out stadiums from Atlanta to Kingston, Jamaica. At the Minneapolis Metrodome, the tour packed in forty thousand people in a single evening; the wait for autographs after the altar call lasted three and a half hours. (Last year's X Games, the World Cup of secular extreme sports, drew only sixteen thousand to a skateboarding competition.) This is big money, big Hollywood skater chic, as different from the Extreme Tour as Jessica Simpson is from Joan Baez. Palau has thrown millions of dollars at the Livin It project, so strong is his confidence in skateboarding as a conversion tool. Skate ramps are trucked in massive glossy black Freightliners painted with a photo of a skater and the logos of team sponsors; these circuit riders travel in a procession of black deluxe campers and vans. Stephen Baldwin never travels in these vehicles—he flies to each event.

To witness Livin It at its most intimate, I meet up with the tour in Sayville, Long Island, just down the sound from where the Baldwin boys were raised. Sayville is a perennially uncool town, where mediocre oldies bands play the annual summer fair on a main street that's *actually* called Main Street. When the tour's überhip skateboarders arrive, all trim chests and shaggy hair, it's clearly the coolest thing to happen since Joey Buttafuoco was convicted. The town is about as mad for Stephen Baldwin as one can imagine people being for, well, Stephen Baldwin. Families gather on every street corner to coo around the lampposts plastered with posters for the event, wondering aloud, "*Which* Baldwin is he?"

Instead of the usual stadium setup, tonight Livin It is appearing at a nearby church. A giant white tent shelters skate ramps and endless rows of folding chairs, which cannot hold the crowd of kids and parents who spill out beyond the tent poles. Baldwin—a slightly different figure from the one you may remember from his slimmer, blonder days—jogs out on-stage, his Jesus T-shirt billowing, his hair slicked across his scalp and down the back of his thick neck. "Yeah, yeah!" he yells over the music. "There's a new Jesus in town, and that's what he sounds like! Are you ready to get *gnarly*?"

Baldwin launches into what appears to be a hackneyed impersonation of what many youth-group survivors would recognize as embarrassing Pastor Cool, mixed with the self-promotion of a fading celebrity. "I've made sixty—that's six *zero*—films in fifteen years. Now I know God intended that so he could use me to do precisely what I'm doing now," he says, pacing and posing. (It may be less difficult to imagine that Jesus Christ was the Son of God if you can believe that God was responsible for the movie *Bio-Dome*.) "The experi-ence I'm having with Jesus Christ has given me the idea to proclaim myself as Stephen Baldwin, the next member of the new movement. You've heard of Jesus freaks? Well, I'm the first Jesus psycho!"

Young mothers swoon alongside their whooping fourth-graders, who hardly reflect the rebel identity these skaters represent. "Now everyone either skates or wears skate cloth-ing or listens to the music that's in skate videos—even Nike makes skate shoes," Shawn Plimmer, the Livin It tour man-ager, told me. "Everybody's converted to skating." When I asked him sincerely what draws the huge number of non-skateboarding girls to events, Shawn looked at me like he could not believe he had to articulate the obvious. "Uh, girls *love* skater boys?" There they are in the front row—all tight jeans and pink T-shirts, eyes wide and expectant for the ricochet of young bodies to begin.

After several minutes of Baldwin's surfer-dude pseudorevivalism, the skaters begin to loop their willowy frames along curves of plywood and rails of steel, tracing arcs in the air, flipping their boards under confident feet. They're pretty astounding, far better than the well-intentioned Extreme Tour guys, and the kids who have taken a valuable evening away from improving their video game scores know the difference: they're starstruck. After the demo is over, Stephen Baldwin takes the mike once more to command, "Come up here right now. The team wants to pray with you." It's no wonder the stage overflows with the eager bodies of hundreds of boys, all filling out decision cards with tiny yellow pencils, hoping that their shoulders will be the next under the grasp of the praying skateboarders. There's no Extreme Tour–style personal connection here, no coffeehouse discussions, no spilled tears. With each card collected—*ka-ching!*—Livin It just adds another saved soul to its elongating roster, packs up the Freightliners, and shuttles on to the next city of anonymous young faces.

If you're a kid on the other side of the American culture line—the one that still wears jeans high and neat instead of low and torn—you can find Jesus riding barrels at a rodeo instead of rocking board slides at a skate competition. I saw eight people claim Christ as their savior one night at the Cowboy Church in Amarillo, Texas, after a death-defying bull ride in the church's newly built rodeo arena. That same night similar events occurred in Nashville and Colorado Springs, and likely at the dozens of other cowboy churches that have sprung up all over the country.

The next night in Dallas, I hung out with the Christian Wrestling Federation during their Bible study, in the ring, no less. Their altar call follows a fully costumed wrestling match in which characters named Apocalypse and Storm persecute heroic Jesus Freak—eat your heart out, Stephen Baldwin—in a seemingly impossible underdog battle; the federation has converted thousands in the past several years. From Dallas you don't have to travel far to come across a Nascar or minor league baseball prayer rally, and you can follow these evangelists all the way out to the West Coast surfer ministries, back through the Rockies, and into New England, to find snowboard ministries, not to mention the hundreds if not thousands—literally—of Christian indie and mainstream rock shows going on every single night with a mission to keep young people steadily enlisting. It's the same basic concept that fires Acts 29, which plants the Mars Hill orthodoxy throughout the country's subcultures. Just as Mark Driscoll trains pastors to bring their culture into church, and just as Dwight Moody preached 150 years ago, so these evangelists are bringing church into their cultures.

What new converts sign on to is hardly just a "personal relationship with Jesus," as they are so often told. To remake one's life as an Evangelical Christian is not just a question of private faith, nor does one's social duty merely adapt to "spreading the Word," as Paul Anderson says in the *Livin It* video: "If you were stoked on skateboarding, you'd say, *Hey, dude—skateboarding!* It's the same thing." It's not. Whether riding a skateboard, a bronco, or a bus to the mall, these new soldiers of the faith must take a scalpel to the flesh of their identity, their politics, and their view of the entire non-Christian world and surgically reinvent what they stand for, privately and publicly, inside and out. But don't try to pigeon-hole them. If skateboarding circuit riders alone can support a spectrum broad enough to include both Ted Bruun and Stephen Baldwin, and venues that range from Council Bluffs, Iowa, to the shadow of the U.S. Capitol, just imagine how this movement makes meaning of the world beyond the half-pipe.

4

In the Name of the Father

The bartender isn't here yet," a woman with a shaved head tells me at the entrance of the Masquerade, a rock club in Atlanta, "so you'll wanna go downstairs." I wander past satin-lined coffins opened to reveal life-sized demonic corpses, and heave open heavy wooden doors onto a dungeonlike space, all red lights and stone walls, the smell of stale beer and cigarettes pungent in the air. The club is divided into three levels: Heaven, Purgatory, and Hell. At the entrance to Hell, a doormat announces, REVOLUTION: DESTROYING RELIGION SINCE 1994. I'm here for church.

The pastor of this congregation is Jay Bakker, the living embodiment of the religious right's worst nightmare. Jay is the scion not just of the modern age of televised evangelism, but of its most damning scandal, which threatened to bring down the electronic church. His father, Jim Bakker, became notorious in the wake of his affair with church secretary–cum–*Playboy* Playmate Jessica Hahn and was jailed for fraud after begging millions from his television viewers.

Jay's congregants perch on folding chairs and bar stools, juggling cocktails, and cigarettes, along with Bibles plastered with Revolution skull stickers. The new U2 album plays before the service—unbeknownst to millions of secular fans, for decades U2 has been the Christian band of choice; just take another listen to your *Unforgettable Fire* LP and you'll hear the message. Bobbing his head to the music, Jay is all dark eyes and prominent eyebrows, the image of his father in generational contrast. It's his father's slight body I see pictured through a scrim of tattoos, that generous made-for-TV smile now pierced with a silver lip hoop.

Rolled up and tucked into the back pocket of Jay's jeans is a magazine called *Sojourners*—the *Nation* of the Evangelical world—which applies faith to political issues in the name of social justice. *Sojourners* is edited by a Christian writer and activist named Jim Wallis, whose best-selling book, *God's Politics*, has secured him a regular spot on the pundits' panels of the secular airwaves, rather than the Christian networks Jay's father once called home. Lodged somewhere between the secular left and the religious right is a marginalized group of progressive Evangelicals; Wallis is their leader. He summed up his frustration of our binary political spectrum in his 1995 book, *The Soul of Politics*—"the critical link between personal responsibility and societal change is missing on the left. Conservatism, on the other hand, still denies the reality of structural injustice and social oppression"— hinting at his own group's homelessness in the polarized dialogue.

Jay Bakker wouldn't articulate his own political position in these words, but listening to his service this evening, it's clear he finds himself in a similar place. Sadly, Jay is the only person I have met in my travels through Christian America who conjures Wallis directly or otherwise—almost no one I've gotten to know in this movement has even heard of this figurehead of Christian social justice. While Jay's pierced lip is an unlikely mouthpiece for Wallis's ideas, he is as much an inheritor of the *Sojourners* ideals as he is of the *700 Club*'s mantle, transmitted not through an analytical or even particularly articulate lecture this evening, but by the whole of the church he has assembled for his generation.

The guest speaker Jay has selected for the evening is someone who would likely hasten a call to security at most Evangelical churches: a big-bodied, short-haired, straight-talking lesbian—her rainbow pride necklace and matching girlfriend complete the picture—who is here to speak about AIDS. Her message is not about the love of Jesus Christ, but simple awareness of this ongoing plague. In graphic detail she dissects the risks behind oral, anal, and vaginal sex in a lecture that stabs at the very heart of the Evangelical movement. "Can you believe it? At schools I'm supposed to not mention condoms because of abstinence-only education—which, by the way, doesn't work," she tells the congregation with a wry laugh. Over three quarters of kids who make abstinence pledges will have sex before they marry, she says, "which I don't care about, but they are taught that condoms are bad so they end up with HIV." Listening from a bar stool off to the side of his gathered followers, Jay applauds vociferously in support of her message.

Jay thanks her and takes his place in front of his parishioners. His sermon is maybe the last thing you'd ever hear on the family-friendly *PTL Club*. "You might say they talked about condoms tonight! They talked about oral sex!" he exclaims. "That's right. That's reality. If this made you uncomfortable and you don't want to keep coming to Revolution, we'll help you find another church. But you should know that Christian kids are sleeping together. They're having anal sex because they think God doesn't look there. Seriously. That's life. People do drugs. People have sex. And I'm afraid if we don't live in the reality of this world, we're just losing the battle."

His words are an in-your-face translation of Wallis's own central criticism of the Evangelical establishment: "Personal piety has become an end in itself instead of the energy for social justice." In a generation of Christians who aren't exactly biding their time in bookstores, this idea needs to be refracted through the voice of someone who looks and talks like Jay, who will present it in raw emotion in front of a rock club backdrop, connecting a progressive Christian mentality with the relational and culture paradigms of this movement. "*This* is the work of the church. *This* is where I want to go with Revolution. *This* is the heart of this ministry," Jay continues, wrapping up his sermon by inviting the entire church to go to the local clinic to get tested with him that week—he's nervous now about the needles used for his latest tattoos.

"Tonight we became a church—a church headed in the right direction," he says, moving himself to tears in front of his small flock, just as his father did so easily twenty years ago before viewers across the world. The notion that this convention-smashing evening constituted an Evangelical "church" is fitting from a man who has worked for only one major institution before—the Gap. Jay's prepastoral experience exactly follows the formula of VH1's *Behind the Music* plot line. He grew up on camera, discovered drugs and alcohol hard and early, dropped out of school, ricocheted perennially between twelve-step recovery and one-step addiction, and found redemption. In Jay's case, redemption came at a ministry camp where he met two Christian counterculturalists who introduced him to the concept of subculture ministry. They admired his first tattoo, which his father abhorred; it said REVOLUTION. That night, a church was conceived.

But it's not the Christian counterculture Jay credits with providing him the heart and soul for this sort of ministry, it's his fallen father and his mother, Tammy Faye, whose emotionalism and mascara-caked fake eyelashes have made her a gay icon. Though Revolution is a clear backlash against his father's neat packaging of Christianity on television—on Bakker's Praise the Lord network one would never dream of hearing tonight's guide to using Saran Wrap during cunnilingus—old PTL broadcasts offer a precursor of Jay's deeply anti-institutional theology. It was the old lights like Bakker who generated the transformation of religion from a Sunday requirement into a twenty-four-hour existence. During a 1974 show, Jim Bakker looked deep into his camera and told his viewers, "It's not a drag to be saved. It's not a boring thing. That's religion. You see, you've got it mixed up. Religion is dull and boring most of the time, but Jesus is life."

The forefathers of the Disciple Generation are yesteryear's dusty pompadours weeping through their pledge appeals, which today make many identity-conscious Christians shrink at the "Evangelical" moniker. James Bakker would tearfully end each of his shows with the pledge telephone number (1-800-CALL-JIM) blinking perpetually across his suit jacket—it's impossible to picture Jay in lapels on-camera or off. The inauthenticity that young Christians today strain against isn't just the product of the secular corporate world, but the antecedents of their own movement.

This sort of quintessential American evangelism has led many members of the Disciple Generation to despise the notion of religion. Jay's own weekly sign-off signifies this shift: "God, help us not to crumble under the bullshit of religion," he prays. The motto of Revolution ministries is *Jesus is the Savior, not Christianity*. It's not his father's faith Jay abhors, it's the way his faith is warped by its institutions, whether inside a cathedral or a television set. It's the institution, he says, that would never allow a speaker like tonight's AIDS activist into a church, and that leads otherwise "good" Christians away from social justice ideals like those of *Sojourners'* Jim Wallis. But Jay is unusual; rarely do young Evangelicals blame Christianity's institutions for their lack of progressivism. It's the hypocrisy of scrubbing clean for Sunday services and wallowing in human sin come Monday that infuriates this generation with all the angsty passion of a freshman-year Marxism student yelling at his bourgeois parents over the dinner table.

Just as the sixties generation rebelled against the practices of their fathers, so does the Disciple Generation. However, the heirs of the old movement, like Ryan Dobson (son of

James, the nation's loudest "family values" voice) and Wil Graham (son of Franklin and grandson of Billy, the prince of the royal family of evangelism), tend to preserve their fathers' faith. But they do so with their own rebel yell against dated mass-market techniques, manipulating their culture in the service of salvation.

In every awakening, a shift occurs between the old lights and the new ones who must anoint faith with the elixir of authenticity before it can disseminate through a generation. For some of these new lights today, it's not just faith that becomes reframed, but politics. Some of the sons of famous pulpiteers take their mission in a direction that would horrify the relatives, others merely dress up their father's right-wing agenda in a hipster coat of many colors. All of them are the inheritors of modern-age altar calls, but despite the marquee last names of these leading soul savers, this is defiantly not their fathers' electronic evangelism—and Jay Bakker would be the first to tell you that.

As much as anyone outside of the indomitable Billy Graham, James Bakker represents what Evangelical Christianity means to post-boomer America. Before the tabloids were set afire by his indiscretions, James Bakker was a principal catalyst of the electronic church, using television as a mouthpiece to convert the masses. Bakker created the *700 Club*, still perhaps the most powerful of the Christian broadcasts today, and beamed his Praise the Lord network from the heavens via satellite into 20 million homes, twenty-four hours a day, on twenty-five hundred television and radio stations. The television empire began with a small on-air puppet show; in spite of Bakker's scandalous end, the network he founded remains the vanguard of the so-called family programming now synonymous with Jesus' airwaves.

Christian broadcasting is as old as broadcasting itself, dating back to the twenties. In the fifties, Billy Graham began the early stages of our current awakening when television cameras captured both his crusades and the souls of his viewers. Graham was the first—and many say the best—to reach out to the American public through a glass screen, identifying the ills and fears modernity had sown in the hearts of men, and promising healing through old-time religion. His altar calls may have led thousands each night to claim Jesus as their Savior in person, but he reached additional millions in their own homes.

Oral Roberts extended the electronic church when he staged the first church services on soundstage, but it was Bakker who truly connected it to the larger culture by developing the first Christian talk show for Pat Robertson's nascent network, taking the church into a secular format—hitherto the hallowed ground of Johnny Carson. In this move, televangelists truly redefined the Christian American, shifting salvation from the meetinghouse—even a televised one—into the den. It is their recent history of slick programming promising miracles in exchange for donations that the current youth movement rejects and distrusts: the notion that faith can be sold like a crystal trinket on the Home Shopping Network. With its hunger for an experience that feels gritty and true, this generation is sick of being treated like mindless consumers. Its broken record plays the same refrain coast-to-coast: *it wants authenticity*. And often, authenticity takes the form of reckoning.

To their parents it might seem like blasphemy, worshiping at Jay Bakker's church in a place called Hell—but that rebellious twist only deepens the appeal. It's also where most people probably feel they belong. Our media-saturated and style-obsessed culture makes everyone an outcast in a way that was never possible before technology ushered in an era of endless television networks flickering with surgically altered bodies or images of war and poverty. Almost none of us *look* good enough and almost none of us *are* good enough to feel redeemed on our own. We are all pariahs. And in our confessional era, when our best sellers are memoirs of misery or self-help books, and Nielsen's numbers skyrocket when sobs shake Oprah Winfrey's couch or the sets of so-called reality television, our brokenness becomes our central identity.

When Jay Bakker wrote his autobiography of surviving scandal, addiction, and depression, he included the following message in his introduction: "If you've felt broken, lost, like an outcast, rejected by God, as if God hates you, rejected by the church, rejected by the world, alone and devastated, and as if no one understands you, this is a book for you." Likewise, this is the movement for you. No matter who you are, no matter who you voted for, no matter how your parents raised you, chances are you could check off one of Jay's dejected boxes. It's just a question of how to pull you in. James Bakker's televised tactics would never seduce this media-savvy generation. They need stealth pop, tangible hip, something that can compete with the flashing colors and insouciance of the secular world. Unlike their parents, they don't want to be sold religion. They want to be sold *lifestyle*.

"Your lifestyle should be the loudest thing you have to say," Cameron Strang tells me. Cameron is the thirty-year-old president of the Evangelical lifestyle brand Relevant Media, and the Disciple Generation's publishing magnate. Unlike Jay, he has no interest in turning his back on mass-media-generated mass conversion; like Jay, he is the iconoclast heir of a pious dynasty—his dad is Stephen Strang, the mustachioed Rupert Murdoch of Christian America. Strang Communications publishes seven magazines monthly and a hundred books yearly, including the first book on the president's Christianity, *The Faith of George W. Bush*. Cameron's company is an indie-label version of his father's corporate empire: alongside a spate of pithy, well-designed books, and a magazine which is the Christian *Rolling Stone*, Cameron also runs Relevant Apparel, which sells hip, seventies-style T-shirts that bear ironic messages like "Bible Thumper" to differentiate their ilk from the elder Strang's conservative suburban marketplace.

Cameron is relatively clean-cut for the Evangelical hipster crowd—his dark hair is sensibly barbered, his arms bear no immediately visible tattoos, and only a small silver hoop hangs in each ear. His boyish cheeks rise and fall continuously between a slight scowl and a gleeful smile, depending on whether he's talking business (scowl) or anything else (smile). Cameron's magnetism is indisputable—just ask his wife, whom he charmed first into a date when she was waiting on his table at TGI Friday's, and then soon thereafter into a church, where she was born again. He has quickly emerged as a celebrity among the young Christian population. Across the country, when people who know him only through the editor's letter he writes for *Relevant* magazine learn we've hung out, they pump me with personal questions, like when I mention Mark Driscoll. Leadership within the Disciple Generation is nothing its members take lightly, especially when people feel these leaders truly understand them.

Cameron and I meet on the 150,000-square-foot main floor at the Denver convention center at the International Christian Retail Show. Thousands of flashy sales booths pitch Bibles and self-help books as far as the eye can see, but in the center of the floor, a crowd thrums constantly around a booth that looks quite different from the others—all corrugated steel and video screens looping footage from Cameron's latest venture, an Internet television site. The booth, new this year, is much smaller than the long-established one beside it, a twenty-foot wood veneer display capped with Cameron's last name. But it's Cameron's booth that's mobbed, while the chairs in muted fabrics at his father's booth next door remain empty.

When he was eight years old, Cameron lifted up a Bible, scrutinized it for a moment, and declared that it would be a much more effective book if it had a better cover. Cameron's desire to run a publishing company is no surprise; when he was growing up, his dinner table hosted the nightly wrap-up meeting between his parents, who run Strang Communications together. But when Cameron announced five years ago, just a few years out of college, that he wanted to start a magazine, he was adamant that it be a very different magazine from the ones his parents publish, each of which caters to their generation and its Christian sensibilities, driven by different passions and motivations. The Strangs told their son they supported him, but he was completely on his own. Cameron took whatever money he had, amassed a stack of credit cards, and began to develop a magazine on a shoestring. It was hardly an instant success. He found himself at Thanksgiving dinner swallowing more pride than turkey; that evening he told his parents he was $250,000 in debt. They did what any parents would do in that situation. They flipped out.

But as loving parents, or as savvy businesspeople sensing an untapped market, they offered to absorb his debt and launch the magazine within their company. He flat out refused. Within weeks Relevant published its first book, a spiritual look at the band U2, which immediately rose to the top one hundred on Amazon.com. The next year *Relevant* magazine debuted with no marketing budget—all it needed was word of mouth. Now the magazine sells out at Barnes & Noble and Borders, and consistently ranks as the top or second-top seller in the Family Christian Stores national chain. Cameron is out of debt, running a company that has quadrupled in revenue each year. In Denver tonight, after the convention floor closes down, he has a date to play poker with ersatz cultural evangelists Stephen Baldwin and Jerry Jenkins, who writes the *Left Behind* series with religious right godfather Tim LaHaye. The key to Cameron's success, and to the momentum of this steadily gathering movement, is to never stray from the mantra *Not your parents' Christianity*.

"My parents don't get it," he tells me. "Their generation is entirely entrenched in church culture. That's where everything happens. They shop at Christian stores. They listen to Christian music on the way to the Christian company where they work every day. They can't talk to someone who doesn't share their worldview." Cameron immerses himself in secular culture with a comfort—and ferocity—the elder Strangs can't imagine; it's what makes him a far more effective evangelist than his parents. "Everything I'm saying about them, *Relevant* is the opposite of all that."

It's also the opposite, he says, of the twenty-something magazines on the secular market, which he describes as softcore porn. *Relevant* maintains the pop culture quotient central to mainstream magazines, but replaces the celebration of tits and testosterone with spirituality. Like the gotcha manipulation of the *Livin It* video—the "sneaky deep" modus operandi—at first glance the magazine appears subtle about its Christianity. Secular stars gaze from behind hip typeface on the cover, and speak and receive criticism within its pages. When teams of kids hired by *Relevant* to pass out free issues recently descended upon Washington Square Park in Manhattan, many people reading copies of the magazine said they had no idea it was Christian until they began to read in depth.

But to secular readers, sussing out Christian content in *Relevant* is like identifying a drag queen with a good wig and wax job: once you know, the evidence is everywhere. A cover story on Moby considers his Christianity in depth; all new albums are rated for their music, lyrics, and spiritual content; an entire section features columnists challenging notions of faith; and nearly all advertising—more hip design—is for Christian schools, youth conferences, books, and music.

Opening each issue is the editor's letter, usually Cameron's direct confrontation to the established church, lambasting it as a "cult of personality" in one issue and "completely irrelevant to American life" in another. "Our generation has a huge crap filter," he tells me, a grin lifting his cheeks. "This approach is what's real to us. People want something bigger than themselves, something with electricity, something they can get behind. And something that isn't shouted through bullhorns or written on pamphlets and handed to them on street corners."

Instead, the idea as Cameron tells me, is to leave an issue of *Relevant* lying on your coffee table so your secular roommate can find it. He'll flip through the magazine to read some record reviews and maybe an artist profile, and then he'll scan columns about God's role in "real life." Drawn in first by curiosity, and then by the writing, he'll end up in a conversation with his Christian roommate about what he read. Eventually, he'll give his heart to Christ. Not because of fire-and-brimstone preaching, or because someone in an expensive suit on television promises paradise, but because an editor shares his taste for bands, video games, and referential humor, and a writer shares his problems. This is the mass media equivalent of outreach in the skate park, or potluck with a pierced peer group: relational evangelizing writ large. It's the "sneaky deep" gateway to a high-decibel Christian lifestyle. *Relevant* has achieved what Cameron's father could never pull off—a way to expand the dynasty into new sectors of the population, affecting far more than their reading habits.

"My parents *are* the religious right," Cameron says.

"Their faith is black and white, strictly cut along clean lines. Our generation is different," he explains, "flexible rather than fundamentalist." Cameron's generation was reared on identity politics and relativism, both of which even Cameron couldn't escape despite the fundamentalist environment of the Strang home. To many members of the Disciple Generation, these mores aid an attitude of Christian tolerance; to others they signify an amoral cancer in contemporary society. Cameron is a good example of a Christian in the former camp. He talks about how his "relative relativism" lends him a Democratic bent, but like most Evangelicals to whom "tolerance" is not a dirty word—though "liberal" still is—he sees his moral center reflected in the Republican Party. The result in the last election was a confident vote for Bush.

Democratic policy may reflect how Jesus lived (or to quote a button my mother gave me when I returned from the Christian front, "Jesus was a liberal"), but it's the Republican Party that invokes the name, if not the teachings, of Christ. The pages Cameron publishes may present different content and design to a different audience from his father's, but when he pulls the lever in his polling booth, Cameron and his father are one and the same.

If Jay Bakker represents the tiny progressive wing of the Evangelical dynasty scions, and Cameron Strang's views tend toward the moderate, aggressively conservative Ryan Dobson tilts the whole spectrum. These guys all look like they should be downing espressos together at a coffee bar in Williamsburg or Silverlake, but with his shaved head, blond goatee, bloodshot eyes, and wicked tattoos Dobson is the obvious alpha male, the self-styled dangerous one. In his book *Be Intolerant*, he rails against the spectrum of despised relativism, crucifying homosexuals, environmentalists, and "inclusive, open-minded Christians," charging his readers, "Get your armor on and take up your cross." He knows just how to instill pride in the heart of his father, right-wing political juggernaut James Dobson.

"As far as my dad and I see it, we look different and we talk different, but that's it. Sure, my dad hates my motorcycle. And he hates these," he tells me, shaking his ornately inked arms that extend from the black sleeves of a T-shirt that says JESUS LOVES MY TATTOOS. "But he bought me my first skateboard when I was seven, so I guess you could say he gave me my first rush." Born and raised in Orange County, Dobson's scene is the X Games world of overworked adrenal glands, organic energy shakes, and sunrises on Mexican beaches. This is no Brooks Brothers conservatism. James Dobson may not take off his jacket at his desk, but so intense is his son's aggro-surfer identity that he doesn't even wear shoes to an interview—you can bet he did, though, when he worked for hard-right moralist Gary Bauer, who founded the Family Research Council with his dad. Ryan approaches the world with the confidence of a leader on the winning team. "I see conservatives like me everywhere, at hot rod shows in Vegas, surfing top breaks on the coast, crazy motocross freaks like me living for Jesus. We know we're right, we have the power of the truth behind us. And because of that, I see cities on fire."

Like many in his generation, Ryan perceives himself as a

preacher not a politician, he tells me, since overt politics smack of dreaded institutionalism. Ryan spends most of his time on the road, at speaking engagements that promote his two hard-line conservative books, or on mission trips that are part evangelism and part sports expedition. He travels with his newlywed wife, Laura, whom he's proud to tell me he married "pure," as though an agonizing celibate courtship between adults could restore his long-discarded virginity.

On this sultry summer evening, Ryan headlines an evening of Christian writers and bands spreading the gospel in Denver's pedestrian district. Publicists pass out temporary tattoos and stickers that say "2 DIE 4," the title of his new book, which challenges readers to "feel the rush" fighting Satan and "the world system" that "brainwashes and uses" Christians. "Our enemy's only goal is to strip your life from you," Dobson writes. "Satan wants us dead. And he hunts us down with a vengeance. Literally." His book is about living like a junkie for the "extreme" life that comes from being a "persecuted Christian," willing to die for Christ at any moment like the martyrs who have perished at the hands of Satanists, because "just like in *The Matrix*, the world contains billions of victims who are all under enemy control." Fighting that enemy, he writes in his book and tells the crowd tonight, gives him the same jolt as his first sky dive. After talking about his own walk with God—complete with anecdotes about evangelizing to mohawked strangers on airplanes and witnessing to surfers as they cling to their boards far from land—Ryan closes his eyes, bows his shaved head, and solemnly prays. "Lord," he intones, "show them where it's at.

Show them the adrenaline rush, Lord." He raises his head, grins, and begins giving away free skateboards to members of the crowd.

As much as a typical Disciple Generation revival might be good marketing for his new book, the global reach of Ryan's ministry isn't through these events, but through podcasting, the medium that has come to represent the vanguard of underground broadcasting in indie culture. Podcasting allows anyone with a laptop and a microphone to spread the gospel internationally; at every minute youth pastors' sermons and post-punk thrash-metal Christ rock are uploaded. It's like radio, but homegrown and self-controlled. And radio is nothing new to the Dobsons.

James Dobson broadcast his first radio show in 1977 from a makeshift studio in Arcadia, California. Thirty years later, Dobson's studio is the centerpiece of his eighty-one-acre Focus on the Family campus in Colorado Springs, where it's the city's second biggest tourist attraction, with its own zip code and exit off highway I-25. Dobson broadcasts to 200 million listeners daily in ninety-nine countries. His radio show is an open mike onto his ultraconservative views on parenting (children should be spanked until they cry), reproductive rights (abortion doctors should get the death penalty), and sexuality (gay marriage represents the downfall of civilization and its proponents are as great a threat as Hitler was), all with the slickest radio production money can buy.

Ryan's podcast is the Disciple Generation's answer to his father's airwaves. Podcasting feels more real, Ryan says, because of its low production values. He amps up those values on his show, answering his cell phone, having conversations off-mic. Its makeshift rec-room sound is what he says makes his message seem—and here's the buzzword of this generation again—more "authentic" than his father's programming. Ryan would rather discuss the giant waves surfed on a mission trip to Morocco during an interview, sure, but his politics are an undercurrent in each broadcast. As a newly married man in his mid-thirties, Ryan admits he's begun to take the implications of his faith and his power more seriously. These days he is thinking of using his downloadable ministry to form a new Focus on the Family, which is more in line—and online—with his generation, reflecting both his culture and his views. "I *bleed* conservatism," Ryan tells me. "It's the center of who I am."

Skaters and musicians—with a requisite appearance by the ubiquitous Stephen Baldwin—tend to be Ryan's on-air guests, but visiting his folks in Colorado on April 18, 2005, Ryan asked his father if he could give his listeners an ear onto Dobson family politics. On the podcast, Dobson père discussed "the battle of all battles," or how "the judiciary is destroying this great nation, and threatening religious freedom and the institute of marriage and the sanctity of life, and, in essence, the entire representative form of government." This, he says, is part of "a forty-year campaign against people of faith," which began in 1962 when school prayer was ruled unconstitutional. "That's not in the constitution! That's not written there! They made it up!" he cries into his son's Macintosh microphone, to Ryan's fawning approval. What he apparently believes *is* written is that "*it is unconstitutional to suck the brains out of babies!*"

Ryan tells me he's especially proud of this conversation.

Decrying fetal brain sucking is apparently where he'd like to take his ministry, but on his own terms, he says, not his father's. Rumor has it that James Dobson is grooming his son to take over Focus on the Family when he retires in the coming decades, but for now Ryan scoffs at the idea. He wants to have the same power as his father, for the same purpose, but no one he knows listens to radio, or digs the starched, disciplinarian vibe of his dad. His role will be to translate his father's message—that Christians must have dominion over the earth and its governing systems—into his generation's language. And while Ryan says he has no designs on political office himself, it's not hard for him to imagine the day when he regularly counsels a president as his father does today. He'd be stoked for that.

——————

For all the Dobson family's influence, there is no real competition for the title of Christian First Family. One name is and may always be synonymous with Evangelical America—the name Graham. It has been noted perhaps thousands of times that Billy Graham has acted as spiritual counselor to every president since Eisenhower, and yet he has never engaged politics from the pulpit or, according to countless articles about him, within the corridors of the White House. His faith has been suprapolitical; he has always known his potential political power and has opted to remain outside the fray. As early as 1952, during a revival he held in Washington, DC, in the midst of a heated presidential race, Graham said, "If I could run for president of the United States today on a platform of calling people back to God, back to the

Christ, back to the Bible, I'd be elected," but among the existing candidates, Graham refused to make even a public endorsement. Such was the separation between church and state back then—a wall built upon the notion that while faith and politics may privately inform each other, it would only poison each to integrate them.

Billy's son Franklin has not hesitated to announce decrees of political archconservatism; he has said he deems it his duty. Franklin was the original iconoclast evangelist, the precursor to the Disciple Generation. He turned his back on the family business, preferring liquor to succor and Harley-Davidsons to holy dominion, but eventually he found faith in his father's God and took up his inherited trade—in a motorcycle jacket. From his pulpit he heaps praise upon George Bush, at whose inauguration he delivered the invocation, and decries homosexuality as a sin against God. When he was asked to give the benediction at an AIDS fund-raiser in New York, he took the opportunity to tell the crowd, "I think it's just as important to save the life of an unborn child as it is to save the life of a man or a woman eaten up with AIDS." Like father like son: now Wil Graham wishes Franklin was more politically aggressive, and whose views—and lifestyle—make his conservative father look at times like a bona fide beatnik.

Wil is a pastor in his late twenties at a white-steepled Baptist church near Raleigh, North Carolina. Today he sits in a navy blue polo shirt behind a gleaming wooden desk in his office decorated with framed pictures, like a snapshot of Dan Quayle shaking Wil's hand, and a head shot, framed and signed, as though to a prominent fund-raiser, of his "granddaddy." This could be the office of a sixty-year-old—there's no iPod charging on the credenza, no skateboard leaning against the coatrack. "I guess I've got guns and bows where the rest of those guys have got skateboards. I guess Ted Nugent is a good combination of both sides of my generation," Wil says, referring to the grizzled seventies guitarist who is better known these days as an NRA poster boy and author of the best-seller *God, Guns, and Rock 'n' Roll*.

Wil's form of relational evangelizing is his attempt to bring heathens to Christ by firing off guns in church. A month ago, Wil and a bunch of good ole boys were shooting in the fellowship hall when he accidentally fired on the elevator shaft. Apparently, the elders didn't mind. "They know I do this because I love Jesus," he explains, eyes dark and intense below the prominent Graham brow. "What else do you love?" I wonder aloud. "Well, I love Nascar. My dream was always to meet Dale Earnhardt, but he's dead now. So I guess I'll just have to settle for my other dream, meeting Sean Hannity." Wil launches into a monologue befitting Fox News's most popular right-wing expositor, about his brother's Christian calling in the U.S. military and his idolatry of President Bush's faith-led policy. "People wouldn't respect him if he wasn't a Christian, just like they wouldn't respect me. Politics and religion have to be mixed," he lectures me, gesturing with a new vintage of his grandfather's giant hands. "Government is God's tool and God's instrument." Wil's model for understanding the relationship between politics and faith is best understood, he tells me, through the work of the Moral Majority lobbying group, run by the man he calls "Uncle Jerry" Falwell.

In a high school where half the student body belonged to the Fellowship of Christian Athletes, Wil was a leader—the best Christian of all. College is *rumspringa* for most good church folk, but at Uncle Jerry's Liberty University, Wil would go to sleep at nine o'clock every night and wake up at six o'clock every morning. He preached his first major crusade his sophomore year. Now at this midsized church, Wil considers himself to be in training—lying low, starting small. He's been trying out his voice in front of the masses on trips abroad with his father, where his preaching gifts appear to be strengthening in the family tradition. This summer he led twenty-six thousand souls to the altar in Gujarat, India, where he preached to ninety thousand people over eight nights. But unlike his father, whose organization Samaritan's Purse focuses its efforts on developing countries, Wil's fires burn domestically.

Wil sees a political revolution gathering force against liberalism, and he intends to be on the front lines. He envisions his entire generation falling in step with his views, whether they're wearing spit-shined combat boots or frayed Chuck Taylors. "We're living in Sodom and Gomorrah today," he intones, suddenly speaking in a preacher's voice, a crescendo building from his abdomen. I glance around me at this Thorton Wilder set of a church office and listen closer for the satanic orgy I must be missing on the quiet suburban street outside. "Homosexuality is praised and honored and Christians are attacked! We praise evil and punish virtue! How can we solve this without a Christ-led government?" I ask him what role he imagines taking in this fight. With his dynastic surname, what he tells me seems as plausible today as when his granddaddy disavowed the same idea over fifty years ago. He wants to be president.

It might seem absurd to imply that gun-toting, Fox-watching, Earnhardt-worshiping Wil Graham could touch the hearts of this largely tattooed movement of young Christians. But therein lies the true revolution behind the Disciple Generation: shared faith links people who would otherwise never be caught dead at the same high school cafeteria table. Profound belief lived out so thoroughly demolishes the usual barriers between subcultures, uniting the least likely people in the same crusade. The demographic cues we use to differentiate ourselves as Americans are secondary to the generation's larger mission: to claim this country, one and all, in the name of Jesus Christ.

eighteen

5

Soldiers of Fortune

E ntering Atlanta's city limits on Highway 20, a billboard greets me. It's a giant image of the famously
bullet-scarred face of rapper 50 Cent, whose debut
album and biopic both carry the title *Get Rich or Die Tryin'*,
which could be the slogan of the prosperity-focused megachurches that pack the surrounding landscape. In this in-
stance, 50 Cent is getting rich pitching Reeboks to the
slowing traffic. But while riches are the frequent subject of
his rhymes, it's not a sneaker company or dedicated fans that
get the credit for his bursting bank account—he's merely
reaping the benefits of his higher calling. *Jesus Christ sent me
to test ya*, he raps.

When, I wonder, did I last endure a late-night MTV
Cribs marathon in which a single B-list emcee failed to credit
Jesus for his in-home theater and white leather sofas? For
that matter, when was the last time an NBA star signed a new
contract without publicly invoking his Lord? Wedged among

the other cars choking downtown Atlanta, I so ruminate while jabbing the scan button on my radio, rushing past the murmuring public radio hosts and scolding preachers at the bottom of the dial, through the hayseed waves of country music, and into the hundreds, where hip-hop delivers the sound track for this and most every other American city.

My car suddenly shudders with the bass line of Kanye West's instant classic "Jesus Walks," whose hook vaulted this secular track into a nomination for a Stellar Gospel Academy music award—a nomination that was retracted after conservative Academy members voiced their dissent. The song's popularity has turned West into an unlikely Christian brand—pictured on the cover of *Rolling Stone* in a crown of thorns atop a visage of *Passion*-style gashes, telling *Playboy* that if the Bible were to be written today he'd surely be a featured "character"—upon which he has capitalized in a smashingly over-the-top metaphor for the rapidly growing movement of "prosperity Christianity." West partnered with the mononymed jeweler Jacob—the hip-hop pantheon's diamond shill named for the father of Israel—in a collection of Jesus pendants that feature the Holy One's likeness in pure gold with tears of rubies and thorns of white diamonds, available for a penance of $50,000. Impresario P. Diddy was not to be outdone by West's expression of faith; he paid Jacob the jeweler $7 million for a 128-carat diamond cross. Once West's track ends, I slip a battered Wu-Tang Clan disc into the stereo and nod my head to the hammering aphorism *Cash rules everything around me*.

Pre-show prayer at the Cornerstone main stage.

Melissa Powell at the Rock for Life merchandise booth.

Moshing against abortion inside the Rock for Life tent.

Stephen Baldwin gets "gnarly for Jesus" on Long Island.

DC Fest

After the demo, skaters pray for the salvation of the crowd.

Kids rush to fill out decision cards committing their lives to Christ.

Ted Bruun leads prayer in a Christian biker bar.

One of the touring rappers feels the spirit.

An Extreme Tour skater tests the ramps.

Rock 'n' roll and tough-love preaching at Mars Hill Sunday service.

Mars Hill Church, in a former warehouse.

Founders Hall at Patrick Henry College.

Morning chapel.

Curriculum highlights at the college bookstore.

Dorm life on a typical weekend night at Patrick Henry College.

Cowboy love in Amarillo, Texas.

Clinton LeSueur schools me
in Christian dominion and
fine catfish in Greenville,
Mississippi.

Good news for people who love
bad news at Focus on the Family.

Lazarus from Goodside.

Friday night worship at New Life Church.

Gordon Harrell's basement Bible study.

The Exalter in the New Life lobby.

Andrew Nagle and students in the science lab at the Christian School of York.

Required reading for biology class.

The Boyett brothers contemplate the Western Hemisphere's largest cross.

It's not surprising that to bring a young flock to the fold, churches today rely on a promise of riches set to a sound track of rhymes and beats. If you're under thirty-five in America—especially if you're black—it's a given that hip-hop is an ethic, an economy, and a code of life, having transcended the street-culture limits of music, dance, fashion, and graffiti art decades ago. But these days, it's not pimps but preachers who slip into custom-made three-piece suits and coordinated alligator loafers. These preachers know that hip-hop, especially when its rhymes promise riches, has the power to draw the masses to their megachurches like teen girls to an Usher concert. The result isn't simply converting new black Evangelicals—rebirthing a nation—but escorting them directly into an increasingly biblical institution: the Republican Party. The holy trinity of faith, finance, and fame has begun to pad voter rolls with a new crop of Southern, urban blacks. These are young people caught up in the split personality the party has crafted of big money and biblical foundations—values that seem less contradictory if you follow the word of popular culture instead of the gospel.

In the city where Martin Luther King, Jr.'s, church expanded far beyond its four walls to include anyone willing to labor for civil rights, this weekend vibrates with the clarion calls of these prophets of profit. Downtown ripples with flags unfurled by the Atlanta Visitors Bureau to welcome revivalists assembled under the auspices of T. D. Jakes, the pastor and best-selling self-help author, and for the next three days the Georgia International Convention Center will thrum with the bass tracks and prosperity messages of preaching phenomenon Creflo Dollar's conference, which he has anointed "The Gathering."

Creflo Dollar—which, astoundingly, is actually his birth name—is perhaps today's most visible mouthpiece of Christian prosperity. You may have glimpsed his precision-clipped moustache during late-night sermons on networks like BET or TBN, or on MTV alongside Jermaine Dupri and Ludacris in their *Welcome to Atlanta* video. Soon you'll be able to see his Christian edition of *Soul Train*, as well as his new talk show featuring episodes like *Old School v. New School*, in which Dr. Dollar demonstrates the bump. Worldwide, Dollar's glossy smile graces the covers of books like *Total Life Prosperity: 14 Practical Steps to Receiving God's Full Blessing*, and the Web site for his online School of Prosperity requires a "Millionaire Login" user name for his instruction on such topics as "Why God wants you to be rich" and "How to increase for kingdom advancement."

Dollar holds the heavyweight title as pastor to the country's fastest-growing church—from zero to five thousand within its first eight months of operation—which meets Saturday nights in New York's Madison Square Garden. Each week Dollar chooses one of his two private jets to commute there from the headquarters of his empire, the eighty-five-hundred-seat World Dome in College Park, Georgia. The Dome is the home church for most of his twenty-five thousand members, including faithful followers such as Evander Holyfield; Diddy and 50 Cent worship with him off-campus.

Several years ago, Dollar famously inspired and supervised

the conversion of rapper Ma$e. These days, when not study-ing under his pastor's tutelage, Ma$e delivers sermons at his own church; I couldn't tell you whether or not they reflect the piety of the lyrics he has recorded since he was born again, like *Put guns in niggas' mouths like "who you dissing?" I pop niggas in the chest, they never breathe again.* Could this man of the cloth mean to imply they never breathe again the air of sinful greed? Perhaps Dr. Dollar has been teaching his charge that Paul was a straight-up thug, too.

Like a true hip-hop star's, Dollar's presence is selective and guarded—he'll appear only once behind his own pulpit at the dome while his "Gathering" flows over into the con-vention center this weekend. In his stead, a youth pastor leads a conference summit about how hip-hop is the indis-pensable tool to make faith relevant to young people. At the summit, compact discs with beats for pastors to rap over are on sale for forty bucks apiece, as are recordings of sermons "on a hip-hop tip" like one called "Realism," which mainly discusses prosperity.

After night falls over the convention center this weekend, hordes of kids in billowing, knee-length T-shirts—many that say GODLOVA—rush into the main hall, essentially an airplane hangar with a large stage facing neat rows of thousands of seats. The seats are mainly ignored by kids, who press against the stage whipping white towels over their heads, like they've seen in so many videos on BET's *Rap City.* A few young guys hold gleaming rims up over their heads, spinning the chrome to catch a revolving spotlight. Pumping up the crowd onstage is a rapper in massive jean shorts and a gold cross that is larger than his head. "The Bible talks about stomping on scorpions, so *lemme see you stomp!*" he yells. "Now lemme hear you scream *Jesus!*"

Another rapper takes the stage surrounded by a gaggle of shaking and grinding women in jeans so tight they appear to form a denim meniscus over each flank. "I wanna know who the crunkers are up in here!" he barks over a screaming crowd. "I heard you were looking for the Holy Ghost, *soldier!*" At the back of the room young volunteers who form Dollar's security force, called Servants of the Lord, stand stiffly, dressed in combat boots and head-to-toe camouflage, their rank tag stating "God's Army." "Are the men of God crunk up in here?" he shouts, to a mass of guys who hoot and whoop in response. "Are the women of God up in here?" The women onstage and in the crowd wave their hands over their heads; if we were in church, their swaying arms would appear to be a show of religious ecstasy. As the conference gains momentum over the next few days, these hip-hop antics will dissolve into the sound of young women wildly ululating in tongues over soft beats on this very stage. Tonight, however, this just feels like a rap show.

———————

By seven-thirty the next morning, thousands of cars have packed the stadium-sized parking lot at the World Dome. A session on marriage has claimed the main sanctuary for the morning, so hundreds of people—slightly older than the crowd at last night's event—line up to board school buses that will bring them to another megachurch just a few minutes' drive from Dollar's massive complex. On the buses, passengers laden with notebooks and Bibles bow their heads and rest their clasped hands on the backs of green vinyl seats, praying together for a fruitful day. What awaits them in the next giant sanctuary is not a worship service or a prayer ministry. This motorcade of packed buses leads to one purpose alone: the day's finance session.

The promise of financial gain resonates deepest with the participants in this session who are too young to have a credit history or significant experience in the work world. They don't yet know that prayer doesn't eradicate racist hiring tendencies, or that in a few years Jesus won't save them when they're turned down for a mortgage. Money in hip-hop culture is the indicator of arrival in a terrestrial promised land, but even in this nation that salivates over cash as its national deficit ever deepens, people can't buy themselves out of racism. Faith is a panacea for all ills in this generation—prayer can redeem a starving bank account, people believe, as it can mend a broken heart or home.

This comingling of Evangelical faith and economics may seem like a uniquely American notion perfectly tailored to our national brand of fervent capitalism, bullheaded optimism, and deist worship of rich celebrities, but its genesis predates the *Mayflower*'s journey. When Max Weber traced the development of the psychology of capitalism, he located its origins in English Calvinism, exported to the New World as Puritanism, which equated piety with work. In nineteenth-century England, Evangelicals began to discuss their faith's relationship not just to work, but to wealth. To these devout Victorians, prosperity—though not its

modern incarnation of conspicuous consumption—was god-
liness; poverty was the cost of an unfaithful, unclean, and
undisciplined life, and was viewed as a spiritual condition im-
proved only by fidelity to the Lord. To believe was to earn.
It's this very notion that propels the expectant crowd into
this enormous sanctuary today. They've come to hear prosperity's promise translated, like every television ad attempting to capitalize on *cool*, into the irresistible language of
youth culture.

Once the seats are filled, a worship leader instructs the
minions to join hands. "We hold hands as our hope that they
will receive that which they came to receive," he murmurs to
the rapt and silent crowd. The smooth, dry hand of the dark-
suited woman beside me actually trembles in mine as she
turns to include me in an optimistic smile and gives me a
tight, quick squeeze of excitement. As I squeeze back, a small,
stocky, and ferret-faced white man in an impeccably cut suit
boldly leaps onto the stage and clambers to the pulpit, confi-
dently running a thick hand through his hair shorn neat and
tight. He's David Avanzini, the son of John Avanzini, the
leading expert on "biblical economics," and he's here today,
he tells us, to lead us to "the finances God intended you to
have in your life." To clarify the authority of this statement,
Avanzini opens a giant Bible at the pulpit and turns to
Matthew 6. " 'Seek ye first the kingdom of God and his righteousness and all this will be added unto you,' " he reads aloud,
words that ignite frenetic applause, the man in front of me
wildly stomping his foot as he pulls a green highlighter over
the passage in his worn and well-marked Bible.

Avanzini's God is Dollar's God, and the very same deity

the late hip-hop icon Biggie Smalls invoked when he rapped that God intended him to have a Bentley. Never in this seminar will the words "all this will be added unto you" refer to spiritual truth, salvation, or eternal life. There is no hesitation or apology in the search for sheer cash—not once does Avanzini flip those slippery pages of his Bible to the unabashed warning in 1 Timothy 6 that says "those who desire to be rich fall into temptation and a snare, and into many foolish and harmful lusts which drown men in destruction and perdition." No, says Avanzini, God says, "I'm a God of abundance." *Amen*. "And you were made in his image." *Amen*. "And so God expects you to have *more* than enough." Across the aisle, a young woman with a bleached-blond Afro nearly breaks a stiletto heel jumping up and down in front of her seat.

Not only should believers hold an expectation of wealth as a mere fact of their faith, but wealth is necessary, Avanzini instructs the crowd, to be an effective evangelist today. Moseying down the carpeted pulpit steps to be level with the audience, he nods slowly to indicate he's about to get *real* with them.

"That gang kingpin? You need to go minister to him," he says. "But you go witness to him in your Yugo and show him what a good God you serve? All he'll see is that Yugo." He grins, pauses a studied beat, and slowly scans the spellbound audience. "You watch that show, you know which show, *Pimp My Ride*. You've seen the waterfall they put in the backseat, and that sistah who got a shoe rack in her trunk. You got so much neon under those cars that when you drive over insects they think Las Vegas has landed."

The crowd guffaws and claps furiously, amen's ricocheting off the expansive ceiling panels.

"You roll up in that, and that kingpin says, 'Where'd you get that ride?' You say, 'My Daddy gave it to me.' "

The whoops and hallelujahs are deafening.

"Then he says, 'You think I can get an introduction to him?' " Another grin, another perfect pause. " 'Yeah, I can get you the hook up.' "

If this were the fifties, the ladies would be fanning themselves and fainting. Instead, the sanctuary trembles with the whoops of a stock rap video. Avanzini saunters back up the steps to the pulpit, straightens his back, assuming classic minister stance, and grasps the sides of the podium. He stares for a moment at the page before him, takes a breath, and bellows, "Seek ye the kingdom of God and all these things"—and now he grins and he pauses for effect—"the house, the car, the bling, the 22's"—he has to yell to finish his amended verse over the hooting and the hollering—"all these things will be added."

How, exactly, the almighty bling is anointed, Avanzini never quite explains, beyond constant emphasis on the need for sheer faith in God and "trust in Dr. Dollar." It becomes clear that the time to express that faith and trust is when the offering buckets come around, while Avanzini says quietly, "Ask yourself, what is it I have that God does not have access to, that might be holding back his hand to ignite everything he has in store for you?" Even when it comes to the will of God, *cash rules everything around me.*

That evening, the World Dome swells to capacity. Many people arrive early to fill the cavernous room with a peculiar din, scattering throughout the stadium seating, standing with arms raised high, their glossolalia breathless and constant. A large woman takes the stage and begins speaking in tongues in front of a microphone, submerging all other sound in her otherworldly voice. She rings a bell and suddenly the room is silent. Breathlessly she chants, "Whatsoever we say and whatsoever we pray is so." The audience—larger than the Southern towns many have traveled from—repeats her words.

It takes seven minutes for the choir of hundreds, cloaked in blue and purple robes, to fill the risers at the back of the giant stage. As they file in congregants sing loudly and boldly, "His report says I am free / Whose report shall you believe? / We shall believe the report of the Lord." Each verse augments the energy in the room as hands pump the air above; now I truly understand raising the roof, even more so when the man standing behind me pulls a tambourine out of a satchel and begins to shake it expertly with all his might. While an elaborate horn section joins in, dancers shimmy onto the stage and strut into synchronized Motown-era choreography, each move captured by one of the television cameras on its own crane, and beamed on digital screens that frame the scene. Each lyric becomes an opportunity for voices to unite in call and response. It's electric; I blink back tears. Everyone in the room—*everyone*—is jumping.

Amid this adrenaline-charged cacophony, Creflo Dollar

strides onto the stage in a blue three-piece suit, and the room explodes with applause. Flashing those sparkling teeth, he stands behind the pulpit, surveys his subjects, and then, like a conductor silencing an orchestra, Creflo bows his head and the room is still. He instructs everyone to join hands. "We thank you, Lord, for the hands we hold," he begins. "We declare for their lives they are out of debt," he commands, rapidly deflating my mood. After some quiet prayers he looks up and smiles once more. *"It's opportunity for prosperity tonight!"*

No time is wasted in passing white envelopes and buckets to collect the offering. Dollar prays over the rustle of opening envelopes and the rip of perforated checks, with closed eyes and a deep, far-projecting voice: "Lord, thank you for the power of anointing prosperity in the area of finances and in all other areas to your people of the Lord." The woman beside me in a threadbare green polyester suit seals her envelope. I hear a deep breath beside me as she bends down to lift a plastic imitation Louis Vuitton wallet from her bag, opens it, and removes the twenty-dollar bill that had been left lonely inside its dark fold. She motions to the usher for another offering envelope. "Thank you," Dollar says. "You are making a mark that cannot be erased." *Yeah*, I think, looking askance at her tense pressed lips, *like a mark on your credit report*.

While Dollar's uncanny name may be the most recognized one in money ministry, scenes like this one play out every week at prosperity churches all over the country. Within miles of the World Dome the prominent self-titled pastor Bishop Eddie Long runs the same shakedown at New Birth, his megachurch on a sprawling landscaped campus in suburban Atlanta. In New Birth's dome-sized sanctuary, where a few months after my visit the memorial service for Coretta Scott King would be held, junior pastors call for $240 pledges to receive a twenty-four-hour miracle. Announcements include the euphoric news that a parishioner broke ground on a gated luxury enclave: "That's holy ground she broke, so you better be preapproved!" Long shouts. Then, in *Price Is Right*–style mayhem, Long gives a new car away to a congregant—*come on down!*

The mania crests when a "fellow brother" is chosen to be made debt-free by church money; a pittance compared to what is to be sealed into envelopes here today, announced as a "miracle from the Lord" that could be yours, too, should you dump all you've got into that white bucket. "That offering will give you a connection with God like never before—a blessing from God you won't have room enough to receive. Think about your brother who became debt-free, just like that, just upon the sound of my voice," says Long. "This says you'll keep the devil away from our finances, that we expect a return on this one-thousandfold!" Prick up your ears on any given Sunday, and you might just hear the sound of bills rustling in black hands all across America.

Dollar relies less on game show stunts like the ones I witnessed at New Birth, and more on the charm of his personality and hypnotic power of repeated speech. How easily the glorious call and response of a sample-worthy gospel hymn becomes something like brainwashing in one of Dollar's sermons. Today Dollar finds his biblical linchpin in the words of John 10. "I came so that they might have life and they might have it more abundantly. They might have it in abundance to the full until it overflows," Dollar preaches from a showman-sized Bible. That the verse is about life, and not wealth, is instantly circumvented—literally dozens of times in the next half hour, "life" is ignored to emphasize words that imply wealth when lifted out of this context.

"It is the will of God for me to live in the overflow. Say 'overflow'!" Dollar commands.

His congregants chant in rich harmony, *"Overflow!"*

"Say 'abundance'!"

A little bit louder now, *"Abundance!"*

"Prosperity is an expression of the love of the Father to his children. It's a Father who doesn't want to see you broke, busted, and disgusted," Dollar rhymes, seasoning his smooth voice, as he often does, with the lilt of the streets. "He wants you to live to the full. Say 'to the full'!"

Fists pump toward the giant dome as people yell out, *"To the full!"*

"Say 'overflow'!"

"Overflow!" the voices boom.

"With this authority and this seed you can dominate! Say 'DOMINATE'!"

"DOMINATE!" The crescendo is uncontainable.

"Say 'ABUNDANCE'!"

"ABUNDANCE!" The room crackles with the will to believe and prosper.

Where is the Jesus who said in Luke 15, "Whoever of

you does not forsake all that he has cannot be my disciple," or in Matthew 5—just one page before Avanzini's selected reading—"Blessed are the poor in spirit, for theirs is the kingdom of heaven"? In Dollar's message we see how the coming of a sandal-wearing, wealth-condemning, intentionally slumming Savior becomes warped in a house of God. His call-and-response routine repeats throughout his sermon, which otherwise touts the value of cultural evangelism and love, but which circles back to these buzzwords promising *Cribs*-style wealth to every congregant.

This brand of Christianity is proven by Dollar's own prosperity. His followers need look no further than his huge gleaming watch that tells him when he should be at an appointment with his personal tailor, or when he should drive one of his two Rolls-Royces to dinner with, say, Diddy or Oral Roberts. In a popular culture that continuously delivers the notion that for black people there is no middle ground between ghetto-poor poverty and garish hip-hop wealth, many people feel they have no choice but to believe. Don't hate the prayer, hate the game: the authority of the Bible offers possibility where little may exist otherwise.

Of course, the anchor of faith is nothing new in black America. Since slavery's days, the church has been community and hope through hundreds of years of hardship. It was faith that impelled the Reverend Fred Shuttlesworth to reopen the Sixteenth Street Baptist Church days after it was bombed during the civil rights movement, and faith that convinced his minions to march right back across the street to Kelly Ingram Park, where Bull Connor's fire hoses blasted bodies with pressurized hatred. Faith is the possibility to believe in the impossible, and civil rights seemed just as impossible to many people in the sixties as their kids' diamond-dripping fantasies do today.

Those dreams surge from the same source. Racial discrimination may have been outlawed since Birmingham's brave boycotts, but for many people the injustice still exists in the form of a yawning income gap. In the same cities where blacks and whites once marched together for legal reform, now segregated pews are filled with young African Americans seeking salvation from earthly inequality. In this generation, envelopes stuffed with cash represent hope for change, every wasted dollar deposited in an offering bucket just one more dream deferred.

After soaking in the morass of prosperity jive during another morning's sessions of "The Gathering," I can't bear to grit my teeth through the lunch sermon. I escape from Dollar's air-conditioned bubble into the thick Southern heat outside, locate my car in the vast acreage of the parking lot, and drive straight to the Sweet Auburn neighborhood of Atlanta, desperate for the meditative equivalent of a long shower. Here, the building synonymous with the civil rights movement still stands, just a few miles from the World Dome: Martin Luther King's home church.

The Ebenezer Baptist Church is a small brick structure, where threadbare stairs lead to a small sanctuary of worn wooden pews. The space feels like a dollhouse chapel after my time spent in the Dome, utterly tiny by the standards of today's megaplex-sized churches. I take a seat in a pew at the back of the musty, empty nave—which couldn't hold the World Dome choir—and listen to the recorded voice of King orating his famous speeches. His Nobel Prize acceptance address reverberates from speakers above the empty pulpit, in high contrast to Dollar's conceit of what faith can achieve: "I accept this award in the spirit of a curator in whose eyes the beauty of genuine brotherhood and peace is more precious than diamonds or silver or gold."

Poverty and social welfare have long been moral concerns at the heart of the black church, and have squared largely with the professed concerns of the Democratic Party; the notion that the "moral values" vote has become a code word for a Republican vote baffles me. It was because of moral values, "the true revolution of values," as King called his fight against injustice, that he and his comrades battled for equal rights. But today, the new black church aligns easily with the image of the new Republican Party, founded on the dual pillars of wealth and prayer. Call it *What's the Matter with Compton.*

Hip-hop's ice-and-rims mentality draws people into new churches that emphasize a reductive and shrewd reading of the Bible, which is then exploited by the Republican machine. "Rappers and Republicans both understand capitalism: *money power respect,*" Tyrone Scott, a young black leader in Georgia's Gwinnett County Republicans, tells me. "You get the respect you want when you have cash. It's practical. I'm a Christian *and* a Republican because I'm focused on the practical issues of living." According to the prosperity model, to *get rich or die tryin'* you have to be a good Christian, which means you have to follow the good Christian party, spreading the gospel of free markets and school prayer by any means necessary.

Although racial discrimination persists, some people no longer view bigotry as a racial issue, but a religious one. To Nehemiah Jefferson, a young Republican son of Democrats—who planned to run for lieutenant governor of Georgia before Christian golden-boy Ralph Reed announced his candidacy—the political battles of his age center exclusively on Christian rights. "My daughter is nineteen months old," he tells me. "As a Christian she'll be persecuted, so she needs to bear the full armor that the Bible says she should put on to address that persecution. This is the true battle we have now—not Iraq, but the war against unbelievers who will persecute my daughter, as well as our chosen president because he says a prayer before making a decision or gives glory to God in his speeches. This is what black Christians are fighting."

The fight is an increasingly effective one. Ohio was able to swing the 2004 election because black Christian voters increased their support of Bush by seven crucial percentage points. Those same voters, and their brethren across the country, have rallied around the Black Contract with America, which was unveiled by more than a hundred Bush-supporting black ministers at a Los Angeles summit. The document includes such party standards as a ban on same-sex marriage and the privatization of social security, all under the rubric of biblical action. The Black Contract is modeled on Newt Gingrich's seminal Contract with America—the very document that succeeded in ushering in the unshakeable GOP domination of Congress during an era when a black Republican was about as common as a white member of the Nation of Islam. The contract is no Dollaresque paean to prosperity; rather, it's purely concerned with the new "values" market the right has cornered.

It is this effective branding of the party as inseparable from the lessons of the gospel—especially in contrast to those heathen Democrats who have long rallied for affordable housing, decent public schools, and accessible health care—that shores up another contingent of young black Republicans, those who locate their faith not in wealth but in abject fidelity to the Word. Just as prosperity theology hinges on a selective reading of the Bible, so does the sort of biblical morality favored by Republican speechwriters and strategists. By ignoring the central tenets of Christianity and instead overwhelming people with what are essentially extrabiblical hot-button issues, they have drawn the children of longstanding black Democrats away from their family's politics and into their own manufactured fold.

North of Atlanta, I meet Lazarus, a rapper whose right incisor, capped in gold and etched with a prominent dollar sign, seems a matched set with his red "Jesus" baseball hat and the rough-hewn stigmata nail he wears around his neck. Despite what his gleaming tooth may suggest, Lazarus isn't seeking wealth in his Republican vote or his personal relationship with Jesus, the two of which he says are inextricably connected. Instead of promising prosperity, he says, his faith has kept him from it. Lazarus's shot at wealth and fame came long before he was born again nine years ago at the age of twenty-one. At the time of his conversion, he was an All-American-ranked star basketball player at Western Georgia State, courted aggressively by the NBA. As soon as he gave his heart to Jesus, Lazarus abandoned basketball and devoted his life to spreading the gospel through his Christian rap with a group called Goodside.

Highway 75 trails an asphalt ribbon to the North Georgia Fairgrounds in Dalton, where a Kmart provides the only distraction from miles of barns and farmland. This evening the fairgrounds' barns and bleachers will host Goodside as part of a small-time music festival supplanting its usual livestock show. When Atlantans insult one another for being "country," Dalton is the country they're talking about: Lazarus's dressing room here is his car; hay and dirt cling to his pristine red and white high-tops. "I woulda *never* been going broke on a crusade like this if I hadn't accepted the Lord, before I was just a preacher preaching over beats," he says, sucking on a lollipop and shaking his head before his show. He sets up a folding chair in one of the fairgrounds' barns and surveys the audience gathering outside by the stage. Every person here outside the group and their small entourage is white, and judging by their collective dental work, Dalton has about as few full sets of teeth as it does platinum cards.

It wasn't long ago that Jim Crow laws defined race relations in this part of Georgia, and only a hundred-odd years since Dalton was ruled by the Ku Klux Klan, during an era when just about every African-American voted Republican.

In those days, Republicans were the men of Lincoln who had brought about emancipation; Democrats were the ruling party in this part of the state, and the party of choice for the KKK, who ensured their election through terrorist persuasion. This is hardly a stretch of land living out King's dream today, but when Goodside takes to the stage, you'd never know. The white bands that precede the group onstage have failed to capture the crowd's attention with their honky-tonk droning. Even in this hick demographic, hip-hop has the power to electrify an audience; it takes a couple of songs to get the set going, but before long, the bleachers have emptied of seated patrons, the crowd is on its feet, pumping its hands overhead just like the kids at the "Gathering" show. Every song takes its material straight from the Bible—you'll hear none of the typical Christian hip-hop references to conspicuous consumption or even the dance hall *crunkin'-with-Jesus* slogans here. Lyrics in every rap, whether they detail personal struggles or gospel lessons, circle back to the resurrection. "He was wounded, bruised for us / Chastised, despised for us / He was tried, pierced in the side for us," Lazarus spits into the mic over the roar of his sudden fan base.

A thirty-one-year-old with a pencil-thin mustache named Gaudscent—né Darius Dunson—is another member of Goodside, and the group's producer. Gaudscent and Lazarus met in college around the time a Christian friend in common had begun to worry them both about their salvation. Gaudscent's conversion came in a moment of misery when he found himself kneeling and crying on his mother's living room floor. He tells the audience his testimony between songs, rendering himself vulnerable onstage, whispering into the mic, taking deep breaths to hold back his tears. The crowd is silent. His voice begins to boom as his story develops into a crescendo, beats softly underlining his words. Gaudscent begins crying out to his Lord as he presses the mic against his lips and, without taking a breath, begins to destroy the next rap in snarling passion—a message against the elites of the nation, which this economically sidelined crowd immediately devours, jumping and cheering. "Ain't no time for compromises / To the people with degrees and awards / To everyone we say, Christ is Lord," he hollers, his head violently nodding to the beat, his body stone-still.

After college, Gaudscent turned his back on a lucrative record-producing career to found Goodside with Lazarus. "We ain't making no money here," he tells me after the show, describing a lifestyle and mission that evokes the Extreme Tour, not Creflo Dollar. "We make enough to cover our costs from crusade to crusade, enough to harvest souls, but that's it. This is our calling. This is living like Jesus did." Gaudscent's home is down the road from Bishop Eddie Long's bougie cathedral in Lithonia, but he never goes to church there, nor to Dollar's services; he's suspicious of their brand of religion. "The biggest enemy to Christianity is the misrepresentation of Christianity," he tells me, referring to the selective reading of the Bible these pastors employ to keep their seats and offering buckets full. "Ain't nothing more dangerous than truth with a little deception."

Gaudscent speaks with reverence for Martin Luther King, Jr., and the civil rights history of the South, which he says he has inherited as part of Goodside; hip-hop, he says, has the power to inspire people here to rise up again. But Gaudscent is hardly a liberal rapping to be heard in Bush country: like Lazarus, and like everyone else he knows, he's a hard-core first-generation Republican. "There are certain issues I vote for. You know the ones. I vote against abortion and gay relationships and for school prayer. That's it. That's why every young Christian I know voted Republican. It's the only choice. I can tell you there is not a single guy, not *one*, in my church who voted anything but Republican. My faith wouldn't let me do *anything* but," he says.

The Bible makes no mention of abortion, but when I mention this to Gaudscent he says, "I don't know about that, but I do know right from wrong. Abortion is wrong. And men, you know, *together* I *know* is wrong." While the Bible hardly endorses homosexuality, it fails to condemn the act any more harshly than, say, the crime of picking up sticks on the Sabbath. When they look to the Bible to denounce gay practices, Christians call upon Paul, whose literally murderous temper led him to condemn as easily as Jesus forgave. Paul said in Romans, "Men committed indecent acts with other men, and received in themselves the due penalty for their perversion," hardly lifting homosexuality up to dire single-issue status, especially coming from the mouth of the Book's greatest blowhard. The Bible does, however, offer very clear punishment for dozens of other practices, like the death penalty for adultery. In other cases when a person is born with an identity the public deems unsavory, the Bible enumerates very specific policies, like the rule that a "bastard," and his or her succeeding *ten* generations, may not be allowed into a church. For a bit more perspective, just consider a couple of the behaviors that are perfectly permitted in the Bible, like polygamy and parents' selling their daughters into slavery.

I've yet to find any biblical mention about prayer in schools, or hanging the Ten Commandments in any building, much less a court of law, although, of course, there were schools and courts aplenty in those days. These issues are essential to Lazarus's vote, he tells me. All the members of Goodside use these examples to decry "government persecution of their Christian status," as he says. Despite a vague and paranoid defense of free will—even if that will is to impose your beliefs on others—there is no connection in his mind to the free choice of terminating an accidental pregnancy, or marrying your beloved, should the two of you have a matched set of genitals. "The Bible doesn't allow it," he tells me firmly and unsmilingly, unwilling to enter any debate. Such visceral "sins" have successfully hoodwinked a former liberal base, especially here in the South. And the Republican Party has handpicked just the operative to organize such outrage simmering throughout the Delta—a young man named Clinton B. LeSueur.

The day I met Clinton LeSueur in Greenville, Mississippi, he bumped into his old football coach. "Clinton, you done turned Republican on me?" his coach exclaimed with incredulity. LeSueur steeled himself for respectful confrontation. "Just kidding," the coach chuckled. "I'm Republican now, too!"

LeSueur, a lanky, tailored man in his mid-thirties, is accustomed to being recognized in these parts. His father is pastor of Tabernacle of Prayer Overcoming Church of God in nearby Holly Springs, where LeSueur was born and raised. While his fourteen siblings stayed behind in the poorest district of the poorest state in the nation, LeSueur ascended to the newsroom of the *Washington Afro American*, and then to a staff reporter position at *USA Today*. During studies for his master's degree in political science at American University, he worked in the Political Analysis Office at the White House. Then LeSueur had a conversion experience, which had everything to do with Jesus though nothing to do with a shift in religious faith. He was born again as a Republican. And everyone in town was soon to find out: he was coming home to run for Congress.

After ordering a plate of fried catfish at his favorite local joint, LeSueur raises his voice over the oldies trilling from the jukebox to tell me the story of his political makeover. "Until the 2000 election, we didn't have any idea the Democrats supported gay marriage and wanted the Ten Commandments out of buildings. You can vote against putting God's word up in a building? Forget it! It should be in every building! It was a shocker for me as a serious registered Democrat. The strangest thing was it hurt me so bad. I don't know how a woman feels when she's been raped, but that's how I felt when I learned the truth about the Democrats. I was like, Lord, I don't want to be a Republican! But faith changed my whole party affiliation. I had no choice but to spread the word." So in 2002 he raised $97,431 in campaign donations and ran against a beloved and well-funded incumbent, a Democrat—and a Christian—named Bernie Thompson. "Every other word on my campaign was faith in Jesus Christ," LeSueur tells me proudly. He won 41 percent of the vote.

In 2004 he tripled his donations and ran again, but lost once more by 10 percent. This time, however, he had attracted the attention of the GOP, who invited the candidate to be one of the opening speakers at the Republican National Convention in New York. "Friends, let me tell you about my part of the country," he addressed the convention. "It's a place where men and women who believe in God and who believe in the greatness of America work hard to make ends meet. I'm running for United States Congress because I want to help save our district, our state, and our nation. The very foundation of this great nation is Christianity and the firm belief in Jesus Christ." His message of Christian salvation resonated with President Bush, who, with Trent Lott's endorsement, named LeSueur director of the Delta Regional Authority Faith-Based Initiatives, a federal-state partnership covering an eight-state region.

LeSueur's support of the president is nonnegotiable. "I don't care what Bush does. He is against gay marriage and he stands for Christianity in public places, so I'll throw all my support behind him. What anchors me in the party is from faith, not the people but the principles. That's how we'll get the government in position behind God! Lobby people the whole nation around to say we're a Christian nation!" LeSueur begins madly stabbing his catfish for emphasis, coaxing smiles from an elderly couple hunched over burgers, who nod approval at his extremist litany. "Teach children Christian values! Pray before you eat! Get Christian prayer back in school! This can be the Mecca of the party right here!" he yells, pounding the table with a tight fist. "I can make it happen!"

LeSueur is unabashed about exactly what he wants to make happen. He wants an entirely Christian government in Washington, and a legislature that will make Christianity both the national religion and the central governmental tenet from which all laws will flow. He says if the Republican Party can't achieve that goal, he'll start his own party, one he calls the Coalition to Restore Jesus Christ in Government. "Look at this country," he says, gesturing across the street to two churches side by side, lit pink by the swiftly slipping Mississippi sun. "We'd win hands down. Then we could put laws into place just like that."

He isn't talking about winning an election based on the black faith vote. LeSueur has long known what I have learned: that there is a massive tide of Christians of every stripe who have in common a short list of issues that play to their own reductive and unflinching faith, and who are energized, organized, and engaged. This isn't just a question of hip-hop culture. It's a matter of the whitest, nerdiest, most uptight, least culturally savvy young voters, who by dint of their faith are standing hand in hand with 50 Cent clones.

"This is our future," LeSueur says, snapping his fingers and holding my look for a beat. "And that, my friend, *that's* how we will overcome."

6

The Ultimate Party School

If you want to see what LeSueur's vision of government might look like, pay a visit to Patrick Henry College in Purcellville, Virginia. The college was founded in 2000 as a response to appeals from senators for "homeschooled" aides—code for young people who share their Christian right ideology—whose training in American government is filtered through a biblical worldview. In 2004, the year the college graduated its first class of seniors, Patrick Henry could count more White House interns in one season than any other school in the country. That's not incidental; in fact, it's the whole point of the college's founding. Patrick Henry exists explicitly to develop a militia of radical right-wing commandants who, armed with their fundamentalism and debate skills, will march upon Capitol Hill and claim it for Christ.

Minority students here aren't divided by their skin color—in fact, there are no black students on campus at all—but by their experience in a real classroom. More than 90 percent of Patrick Henry students have parents who educate their children at home, for fear that the secular poison of a public school curriculum will infect the faith of their family. Two million kids are homeschooled every year, at an annual growth rate of about 10 percent, according to the National Home Education Research Institute. Before Patrick Henry opened its doors, these kids had no place of higher education that would guarantee that their parents' abject absolutism would be nourished and preserved. There are many Christian colleges nationwide—Cameron Strang graduated from Oral Roberts University, Ryan Dobson attended Biola, formerly known as the Bible College of Los Angeles, and Wil Graham holds a diploma from Liberty University, to name a few. But while these colleges stress the Bible's guidance in the classroom and the dorm room, there is no place quite like Patrick Henry. The codes of dress and behavior here seem to be adapted from the social bans of Calvinist seventeenth-century Massachusetts; in an unusual show of wry humor, one pale and exhausted-looking student told me, "I was thinking about going to Liberty University, but then I thought, *Why should I have any fun?* And my parents were plenty pleased I wasn't going to."

For parents who prefer to keep their kids at home through college, but still want to teach them that the Founding Fathers intended an explicitly Christian nation, Patrick Henry offers a distance learning program, making its fundamentalist classroom a national one. However, to claim the government for Christ, a true soldier must train on-campus at Patrick Henry's four-year political boot camp, fifty miles from the White House. Parents may be reassured by the college's paternalism and Christ-centered curriculum, but that's just the beginning of what happens here—a higher calling *to rule* is what the school has in mind for its graduates.

As the college materials repeat as often as amen's in a Sunday service, these students shall go on to "lead the nation and shape the culture." Since its inception, the college has had much more than financial support from conservative fund-raisers and politicians alike—students and recent graduates have been given unfettered entrée to the nearby corridors of government; even the former dean of academic affairs stepped down to accept a senior level position with the Bush administration in foreign policy. A mandatory and extensive apprenticeship program is designed to get them in the door long before they toss their mortarboards heavenward, landing students in Supreme Court chambers and congressional offices before they ever need to apply for a full-time job. Beyond their internships, nearly every Patrick Henry student campaigns for right-wing candidates. Recently, Senator Rick Santorum came to speak at the college because such a huge number of students helped secure his reelection—the entire student body showed for his address.

Training in the political arts precedes enrollment for most students here; homeschoolers are far more likely to be politically engaged than other youth. Through the past couple of decades, these kids have stood beside their parents in their battle for the right to teach their children at home. From the time they could cut their own food, they've stuffed envelopes, called legislators, and appeared at state houses, personalizing what has been framed for them as a crusade against liberal persecutors. Patrick Henry's founding body, the Home School Legal Defense Association, recognizes the force that lies in this expanding body of activated youth, a force that if organized nationally can push a distinct and familiar agenda through Washington.

"Homeschooled young people will help reverse *Roe v. Wade*, stop same-sex marriage, and help reestablish a strong view of the freedoms established by our Founding Fathers," says HSLDA chairman and Patrick Henry president Michael Farris, a man whose middle age is belied by boyish good looks and junior-senator-style thick hair, and who requires by rule of the student handbook that students call him "Dr. Farris," though he holds no doctorate. Farris scowls derisively at Rock for Life's "ridiculous" notion that change is made through culture; to Farris the victory of this movement lies in classical education geared toward Christian government, which, he repeats to eye-glazing effect, was the intention of the Founding Fathers. Even the art outside his office speaks to this rote lesson—an engraving depicting the first prayer made in Congress, intended as much as a metaphor for Farris's vision as it is a history lesson.

Farris himself has done well in his crusade. He sat comfortably at Bush's arm when the president signed the bill banning partial-birth abortion; Karl Rove's number is programmed on his speed dial. Farris has played key roles in the Moral Majority and Concerned Women of America, in addition to single-handedly mounting and leading the successful legal fight for homeschooling. The only career defeat Farris has suffered was his run for the lieutenant governorship of Virginia in 1993, but that setback was as temporary as a term in office. His losing campaign only fed his motivation, the result of which is the full-fledged political onslaught of homeschoolers he has amassed in the years since.

When Farris considers his young battalions he is reminded of the "heroes of faith in Hebrews 11," he says, " 'who through faith conquered kingdoms, administered justice, and gained what was promised; who shut the mouths of lions, quenched the fury of the flames, and escaped the edge of the sword; whose weakness was turned to strength; and who became powerful in battle and routed foreign armies.' " Farris and HSLDA have developed an apparatus to train these armies from puberty's onset, long before they are old enough to vote, or even take the PSATs. First, homebound high school students sign up for an online curriculum in political organizing, which places them in clubs that campaign for carefully selected "pro-family" candidates nationwide. These clubs also form the volunteer corps—or student action teams—of the new HSLDA Political Action Committee. The volunteer corps directs students in summer camps on the college campus, where their days aren't spent playing volleyball or making God's eyes out of popsicle sticks, but doing intensive political organizing. Older campers are advised to apply to the college, and most of them matriculate as freshmen, often before their eighteenth birthday. It's a brilliant scheme to ignite a national movement and to control exactly what influences these crusaders from their childhood straight through graduation day.

Most Patrick Henry students I've talked to say they've had no non-Christian friends, and many ask me in wide-eyed wonder if life in a regular high school is really like what they've seen in the few teen movies they've been allowed to watch, "like cheerleaders and food fights and everything," one ponytailed freshman clad head-to-toe in powder pink asked me. My mundane account of high school caused her overly made-up face to fall: no car chases as in her—surprisingly—favorite film, *Rebel Without a Cause*, no liaisons as dangerous as those in *Cruel Intentions*; her lifetime of defining herself against an oversexed, undisciplined, illiterate cinescope cliché instantly undone. (Admittedly, I left a few things out.)

Students here joke about being homeschooler proto-types, and watching them walk stiffly to class in unfashionable business suits, clutching Bibles and textbooks, it's easy to see why. One pale-faced junior I pass in the hallway nods and comments without irony, "Some weather we're having," as though programmed to use certain phrases and tones with unfamiliar adults. It's a creepy experience to be surrounded by hundreds of able-bodied, red-blooded young men and women who would be testing the chemical and sexual boundaries of human biology anywhere else. Here, they appear like robots, bred and raised to carry out a mission from God.

The success of their mission is already spectacular. Patrick Henry's debate team trounced Oxford at Balliol College last year—no small feat, especially considering they were arguing English common law. That evening, Farris felt his deepest moment of pleasure not when the judges delivered their verdict but afterward, at the celebration hosted by the college's Younger Society. When Oxford's senior law lords arrived for supper in the Great Hall, alumni all, Farris prophesied a similar future gathering of Patrick Henry graduates. But in his imagination, Farris saw more than just Supreme Court justices, the American equivalent of the lords; he pictured a new group of Founding Fathers whose legacy will be the redefinition of the United States.

——————

Patrick Henry College lies deep in the heart of the developer-razed horse country many Hill staffers call home. The campus, designed by a Christian architecture firm, is the sort of place that photographs well, all traditional brick and white window panes, but in person feels too shiny and hollow, like it was ordered from a catalogue—the "Veritas" package, perhaps—or moved from a Hollywood backlot. In this backward-looking architecture, indistinguishable from the endless McMansions and new churches down the road, a semicircle of dorms faces a small pond, which is pastoral enough if you keep your back to the highway a hundred yards away. Up a slight slope is Founders Hall, where classrooms, the cafeteria, and HSLDA's offices hum behind a portico of Doric columns.

The atrium of Founders Hall is a gallery of portraits of the Founding Fathers in gilded frames; or Christian apostles, as students have come to know and worship them alongside their Lord. Down the hall, a more recent but equally revered image of the LaHayes—Tim, the coauthor of the Left Behind series, and Beverly, the founder of Concerned Women for America—hangs alongside framed plans for a 103,000-square-foot student center. The center will cost $16 million to build, all of which needs to be raised before ground is broken, since Patrick Henry functions entirely without debt, but the college plans to start building within the year, thanks to an aggressive prayer team and a hand in the deep pockets of some of Bush's top contributors.

The school motto here is "For Christ and Liberty," which underlies chapel service today and every day. In the chapel—essentially a large meeting room at the back of one of the dorms—the only icon of reverence is not a cross but an American flag. The student body assembles for compulsory daily worship, girls hidden by long dresses and boys in dark suits, to listen to a pastor promise, "God has a plan for you to take back the land," his language echoing the violent, ruinous words of Deuteronomy 7, which happens to be Farris's favorite Bible verse: *And the Lord your God will drive out those nations before you little by little; you will be unable to destroy them at once, lest the beasts of the field become too numerous for you. But the Lord your God will deliver them over to you, and will inflict defeat upon them until they are destroyed. And he will deliver their kings into your hand, and you will destroy their name from under heaven; no one shall be able to stand against you until you have destroyed them.*

After the assembly concludes a pious round of hymns—I'm a little disappointed that they don't sing "Mighty Army of the Young" (*Lift the cross and sheathe the swords*)—they pray, not for salvation or for a decent grade on a history test, but for God to help "pro-family candidates" sweep the upcoming elections. A floppy-haired student stands to close the service with announcements. "You all know it's just one month before the general election," he says. "The governor's race, as you all know, is neck and neck. So get out your conservative principles and *get moving*! At two-fifteen the vans will be picking us up in front of Red Hill. *We've got work to do!*"

At Patrick Henry the application for admission requires a letter of reference from a pastor and an essay assignment on "your faith in Christ and the role you believe PHC can play in the plans God has for your life," rendering this battalion of eager warriors somewhat self-selecting. This may be typical of a Christian college application, but as the admissions materials consistently assert, this is no ordinary Christian college. To emphasize its unflinching rigidity, there's something else that appears in every student handbook, on the college Web site, framed on campus walls, and printed on the application. This is the college Statement of Faith, which must be subscribed to "fully and enthusiastically," and be signed by every applicant and faculty member—even by kitchen staff. It says:

- There is one God, eternally existent in three Persons: Father, Son, and Holy Spirit.

- God is Spirit, and those who worship Him must worship Him in Spirit and in truth.

- Jesus Christ, born of a virgin, is God come in the flesh.

- The Bible in its entirety (all 66 books of the Old and New Testaments) is the inspired word of God, inerrant in its original autographs, and the only infallible and sufficient authority for faith and Christian living.

- Man is by nature sinful and is inherently in need of salvation, which is exclusively found by faith alone in Jesus Christ and His shed blood.

- Christ's death provides substitutionary atonement for our sins.

- Personal salvation comes to mankind by grace through faith.

- Jesus Christ literally rose bodily from the dead.

- Jesus Christ literally will come to earth again in the Second Advent.

- Satan exists as a personal, malevolent being who acts as tempter and accuser, for whom Hell, the place of eternal punishment, was prepared, where all who die outside of Christ shall be confined in conscious torment for eternity.

To sway from any detail of the Statement of Faith during one's affiliation with the college is to terminate that relationship. Last year, an assistant librarian expressed to a student his belief that baptism, and not mere faith in the Savior, as the statement says, is a prerequisite for salvation. He found himself promptly fired; the supposed liberalism of higher education (literally) be damned. This policy extends not just to belief in the fundamentalist statement, but in the college itself. When I comment to an administrator after class one day that I've never seen a group of students so diligent and vocal, he shoots me a dark look and says, "Listen, between you and me, I haven't exactly drunk the Kool-Aid yet." Within two months, he's no longer an employee of the college.

At Patrick Henry, there's no hard-core band screaming about Jesus at campus parties, no audiovisual club weighing the merits of Robert Rodriguez and Brian DePalma, no student who wanders Founders Hall in spiked hair and a shredded Christian T-shirt. This is a group of deeply focused, unflinchingly strategic movement operatives organizing without the blandishments of rock 'n' roll, taking up the same mantle of Christ as their tattooed brethren, but with access to the highest levels of government. Renegade Christianity has no place at this training corps for the Hill. All the bohemian authenticity that exists elsewhere in this youth movement, all the street slang and fashion, all the Jesus punks who might clasp a pen between black fingernails to sign the Statement of Faith—this world exists far from the student body.

In the sixties, "the system" was the villain. The first step in revolutionary engagement was to divorce oneself completely from established institutions that made up and fed that system: the academy, the government, the power structure. While sixties-style anti-institutionalism is alive and well in the Christian counterculture—at Rock for Life, on the Extreme Tour, at Mars Hill Church—the Disciple Generation attacks from both inside and outside the system. The emergents and postmoderns may be shifting culture from the margins, but they are aligned in the very same fight with the uptight nerds of Patrick Henry. The students here are so establishment-minded that they wrote their college applications with an eye toward admission into the Congress as well as the college. Just as Mark Driscoll plans to repopulate Seattle with its own baby boom, so Michael Farris plans to repopulate Washington, DC, with these students indoctrinated with the politics of the Christian right. It's one thing to proselytize on the half-pipe or at the rock festival, but it's another thing to integrate religious tenets into federal legislation. By funneling its graduates into the governing institutions of this country, Patrick Henry will necessarily effect massive change.

First, though, they have to dress for it. Students must wear business attire between the hours of 8:30 A.M. and 5 P.M., Monday to Friday. Men's hair is to be kept off the collar in the back and above midear on the sides. No piercings are permitted, except for women wearing earrings; no tattoos may be visible. Lunch is at noon and dinner is at five (lots of ham and tater tots are served at both). An Internet program called Covenant Eyes scans and flags students' online habits, keeping a log of all activity to be searched in case of a "problem," or in other words, a porn habit. Television channels like MTV and HBO are blocked from sets, and what's left to see must filter through a "curse-free TV unit," which a few students told me is fine with them, since last year they watched only the presidential debates. If a student is to rent a DVD, in no case may that movie contain nudity, profane or blasphemous material, crude humor, graphic violence, or other aspects of visual popular culture. The student handbook illustration of a forbidden film with nudity is *Braveheart*, which happens to be about a warrior committed to taking back the land; profane or blasphemous material is exemplified by *Bruce Almighty*, which happens to be written and directed by a Christian.

Dorm rules are equally extensive: if you wouldn't tell your parents about it when you were thirteen, you can't do it here. One senior has already worked in Vice President Cheney's White House office and gone prematurely bald, but he's still not allowed to kiss his long-term girlfriend on campus or even enter her dorm room. Like every other student here, until graduation he must court her in a well-lit common room. It's no surprise that the dorms here are essentially odorless—no rooms I visited are scented with the tang of newly discovered sex; there's no stale smell of pot smoke or last night's overturned keg seeping from doorways into the carpeted corridors. Of course, alcohol and tobacco are verboten. A wild party at Patrick Henry involves throwing a pillowcase over a roommate's head, leading her out to the flagpole, pulling off the pillowcase, and forcing her to run around the flagpole ten times singing "Yankee Doodle Dandy." Seriously. In case this wasn't already calling to mind the conservative town immortalized in *Footloose*, yes, there is no dancing allowed.

Of course, with intense academic requirements and most students away from campus each weekend for debate championships, moot court tournaments, or virgin weddings, it's not like anyone has time for partying through the weekend, anyway. When you meet some of these kids—like Kyle Murray with his *Tiger Beat* face and perfectly fitting suit, his easy charm that mitigates a propensity to drop names of major Bush donors, and his impressive Foundation for Defense of Democracies fellowship—it's hard to imagine at least part of the student body not getting it on. But then you talk to them, and most of the time it's like watching young actors in movies from the early forties: prepped out and speaking in preternaturally crisp diction, at once ancient and childlike, fresh from senior year and ready to go off to war.

As was done in the early days of the Ivy League, when each college was still denominationally Christian, government class begins with the reading of a psalm. In Professor Robert Stacey's "Freedom's Foundations" class, today it's Psalm 19: "The heavens declare the glory of God; the skies proclaim the work of his hands." Students bow their heads over Oxbridge-style long wood desks carved with the school seal. As soon as Stacey is done, they open Dell laptops, fingers at the ready to type diligent notes during the lecture. This class is part of the core directed toward teaching students that the United States was founded as an explicitly Christian nation, instilling the rhetoric to wage an aggressive campaign to bring the nation "back to our roots" and to battle modernity, relativism, and liberalism. Stacey and other professors here like to talk about the importance of the Socratic method in their classes, which usually takes the form of asking a student to debate the merits of what is frequently derided in class as what "secular textbooks would tell you," such as the notion that there's a separation between church and state, or a right to privacy implied in the Constitution. When a puzzled silence occasionally falls over these usually eager students, professors nudge them toward the right answer by saying, *Come on, guys, you know the key to this! Biblical principles! Go back to scripture!*

An education that constantly circles back to the Bible is boilerplate for everyone at Patrick Henry, since almost every student here was taught with Christian-centric curricula before matriculating. Many of them used Michael Farris's own *Constitutional Law for Christian Students* in their living room high schools, which introduces students to founding documents and court decisions. *Constitutional Law* teaches that "for Christians these decisions need to be made based on two written standards of higher law: the Bible and the Constitution." The textbook applies the politics of the Christian right to every topic, whether discussing the free exercise of religion ("This case will teach Christians a permanent lesson: People who call themselves 'conservatives' are not necessarily our friends"), abortion ("Death by Penumbra"; "the worst decision ever made by the Supreme Court"), or homeschooling ("We view many laws which regulate home schools or Christian schools as bad 'protection' laws. We are not willing to give up our freedoms to public school regulators who cannot operate their own schools properly"). Farris's curriculum is a classic example of why, unlike at other schools, Patrick Henry kids don't develop political ferocity during their freshman year—it's crafted long beforehand.

Homeschooled kids are fourteen times more likely than the general public to work for a candidate or political party, according to the National Home Education Research Institute. To their families and themselves, politics aren't theoretical. Their very education and identity, for better or for worse, are the living embodiment of hard-won political action. Take Amber Smith, a lanky blond junior—the type modeling scouts search for at state fairs—who is vice chair of the Patrick Henry College Republicans. Amber grew up in South Dakota, raised by a mother and father who were the first to be born again in their families, and who wanted to inoculate against the effects of a godless public education by homeschooling their kids. When Amber was a toddler, advocates in her state won the right to teach their own children, but just across the border in North Dakota, the fight was longer and fiercer. Some of Amber's clearest childhood memories are of family friends taken to court by the state for doing with their kids exactly what her parents were doing with her. All she's ever known is the necessity of political battle.

During Amber's high school studies, she worked with the South Dakota Family Policy Council, which she describes as a state-based organization modeled on James Dobson's Focus on the Family. When she turned eighteen, the state Republican Party offered her a job as a coordinator on John Thune's first campaign against Senator Tom Daschle. At the party offices she worked seventeen hours a day for three months straight; when Thune lost she cried for three weeks. Then she pulled it together and enrolled in a school that would encourage her to take time off to work on Thune's second campaign, this one triumphant.

Amber is one of sixty students at Patrick Henry with a role in the student action program called Generation Joshua. The name comes from Farris's notion that his generation is the Moses Generation, which led its children out of Egypt, or in this case, out of the dark secular morass of public schools. Joshua, successor to Moses, was the leader of the first generation to grow up outside Egyptian tyranny and slavery. As Farris puts it in his book *The Joshua Generation: Restoring the Heritage of Christian Leadership*, the movement will succeed when this generation engages "wholeheartedly in the battle to take the land." This is no mere rhetoric. The Generation Joshua office in Founders Hall runs an online civics education course accessible for a fee of just $10 a year—Founding Fathers, balance of power, the usual "true Christian nation" fare, but this time cut with intensive grass-roots organizing modules—and has just developed a civics textbook.

The meat of Generation Joshua is its clubs, which are local activist groups that each year grow threefold in total (zero to thirty its first year, thirty to one hundred its second), and threefold again in members (fifteen per club the first year, forty-five per club the second year). Beyond the clubs and online curriculum are voter registration initiatives and regular chat room sessions with Generation Joshua president Ned Ryun. Ryun's previous employment was as a speechwriter for President Bush; his father is Kansas senator and Family Research Council darling Jim Ryun, who has exhibited a penchant for speaking in tongues at public events. At the GenJ office, as it is known, Ryun identifies which races are key for the Christian-right cause—where the most conservative candidates are running, or where the most liberal candidates are in a tight race—and dispatches his staff to coordinate operations to bring student action teams from across the country to campaign in each flagged election.

Generation Joshua is essentially the activist arm of the HSLDA PAC; the two groups were established simultaneously in 2003. Farris claims that the central purpose of the PAC is not to raise money for candidates or to gain lobbying influence in Washington, but to develop the proper legal structure for students to work campaigns. Rather than reaching out to political contributors, the PAC Web site exists to give information to the parents of activist homeschoolers. It says, "Rest assured we are going to carefully screen the races in which we ask our teens to volunteer. Only candidates who are pro-homeschooling"—which we know is code for a host of far-right preferences—"favor the original intent of the Constitution, and possess a strong loyalty to liberty and self-government will receive our assistance." The PAC covers all expenses, including food, lodging, and travel, for students who are willing to travel across the country to work for candidates the HSLDA supports.

For the 2005 election, the PAC bused nearly four hundred GenJ members from states like Florida and Ohio to Virginia, where they contacted more than a hundred thousand voters by phone and knocked on more than sixty thousand doors statewide. While the conservative candidate for governor lost the race, sending hundreds of Patrick Henry and GenJ campaign workers into fits of tears, a "pro-family" lieutenant governor and attorney general were elected. HSLDA-tapped Virginia delegate Matt Lohr won his race by a thousand votes—Generation Joshua increased turnout by a thousand in his district. In the 2004 election, every GenJ supported candidate won, with a single exception.

That was the year a soft-spoken, greasy-haired boy named Robert Hogan, now a Patrick Henry freshman, joined the effort. He was the 214th student to sign up with Generation Joshua, he tells me, rolling up his shirtsleeves and proudly crossing his arms over his wide chest to punctuate this declaration; when he talks about his recent political efforts, his adolescent hunch straightens with dignity. Unlike most homeschoolers, Robert had never volunteered for anything before, nor had anyone in his family, whose civic engagement began and ended with watching the nightly news together. Robert's high school curriculum focused on math and science, since this was where his aptitude lay. But the GenJ civil action curriculum intrigued him, and within weeks, Robert was having regular online chats with Ryun about what was going on in Congress that week.

Through the program's activist component, Robert began registering voters in his area, and then traveled to Pennsylvania with other GenJers to campaign in Pennsylvania during election season. He was hooked. His new zeal was infectious: his entire family immediately committed its time to voter registration and conservative activism. That summer he participated in Farris's Constitutional Law Clinic, and then enrolled in debate camp on campus here. Now, as a freshman, this former math geek and politically disengaged teenager is a lead coordinator in Generation Joshua, with dreams of elected office.

To take back the land, a political movement needs more than candidates and campaigners, it needs lawyers and lobbyists, men and women—though in this case mainly men, since women must birth the babies and homeschool them—who will one day wear the black robes of justices on the state and federal level. Obviously the dream—nay, the plan—is to pack the bench at First and Capital Streets Northeast. To this end, HSLDA established the Homeschool Speech and Debate League. Peter Kamakivoole, a sophomore from Oahu who wears an American flag pin on the lapel of his black suit, was active in the league before college. This year, at age eighteen, he became the moot court national champion—that's not just of a Christian league, but the entire country.

Peter speaks with reverence of the Speech and Debate League—vacillating between polysyllables and repeated use of the word "neat"—which he credits for his success. "The focus of this league is different than other leagues, since for us debate is more than debate," he tells me over lunch in the cafeteria. "For us, debate is preparation for life and leadership, to challenge culture and impact government and law." Peter is confident that next year he will land an internship at the Supreme Court. "It shouldn't be a problem; we've already had quite a few," he says. For now he's content with supplementing his studies with work "upstairs" in the HSLDA office and regular moot court showdowns.

Now that Peter attends Patrick Henry, his coach is the college president. At moot court practice in a classroom in Founders Hall, he stands behind a podium and lays out a sharp but gently paced argument for why a church should be able to install a cross in a park, then engages Farris in well-sourced banter about the difference between exercising belief and believing, terminated only by the noon bell. For students here, but especially the 15 percent of students who make up the moot court and debate teams—the Patrick Henry equivalent of Big Ten football—life is arduous and regimented. Here's one day's schedule for debater Rachel Williams, a curly-haired policy major and parliamentary debate star from San Diego:

6:30 wake up
6:45 exercise
7:30 breakfast, study
8:00 class
8:50 study
10:00 chapel
10:40 study
11:00 western world history—quiz
11:50 grab lunch, review debate theory, gather resolutions, study for presidency class
2:00 presidency class—quiz
2:50 review debate theory
3:00 debate meeting
4:00 study in room
5:00 dinner
6:00 study
10:30 bed

This is a relaxed Thursday, since it's one of the few weekends this semester that Rachel doesn't have a debate. Next Thursday, Rachel will climb into a van immediately after chapel and drive eleven hours to the debate site, preparing every minute of the way, carsick or not. It's her last year here, and she must make every moment count. She also works with Generation Joshua, this season focusing on the governor's race; last year she spent weekends between debates campaigning in Tennessee. "The high point," other than winning, "was when a military leader on the campaign taught us how to do the battle cry," she recalls. Next year, Rachel plans to study law at Ave Maria, Regent, or Notre Dame, since those are the only explicitly pro-life legal programs in the country.

Rachel's schoolwork this year has focused on family and society, particularly United Nations policy, Catharine MacKinnon's writing and legal work, and the philosophies and activism of Elizabeth Cady Stanton. I, too, furiously studied these topics as an undergraduate, though at Barnard College in New York, which Rachel and I agree might be the opposite of Patrick Henry. Over coffee, we have a lively and lingering discussion about her papers. She is thoughtful and respectful even when the conversation turns especially frank around the subject of Elizabeth Cady Stanton's vehement rejection of Christianity as an institution that robs women of their most basic rights. It's too clear a segue to pass up. I ask her what happens after law school when she marries, has children, and renounces her work to care for them, as she believes the Bible asks her to do—she, after all, is one of the leaders of the nation's largest debate league, hardly someone using college to earn her MRS. Rachel says she'll stay at home, but continue her work outside the legal system by inviting single pregnant women into her home. A seat on the Supreme Court is not an ambition she can admit to having.

What if Rachel didn't have to sign the Statement of Faith? What if her college permitted, or even encouraged, true intellectual combat with scripture? What if she was permitted to express something other than "full and enthusiastic" commitment to the conviction that "the Bible in its entirety (all 66 books of the Old and New Testaments) is the inspired word of God, inerrant in its original autographs, and the only infallible and sufficient authority for faith and Christian living"? She might still have a deep moral objection to abortion, and might still believe that men and women have different roles, but at least she would have arrived at those principles herself; those ideas would be her own to follow or discard on her formidable path.

Can a young woman as smart and rigorous as Rachel possibly believe what the inerrancy statement literally requires of her? If she believes that every word of the Bible is literal truth, then she believes that, for example, Levitical law is infallible. In other words, she believes she should be stoned to death for disobeying her parents, her future husband should be free to take multiple wives, and any of her friends who may have fallen into bed with a man before her wedding night should be executed. It means that, as Moses said, she should kill me dead, right here in the cafeteria, for my status as infidel.

These thoughts surface again when I meet a different type of student here, the emerging literary heavyweight. While Patrick Henry was founded for the training of political operatives, the college has already grown beyond its original mission and has recently followed the demand to establish a creative writing and literature program. Farris has long said that he hopes Patrick Henry will be the first jewel in a crown of new elite Evangelical colleges, a fundamentalist Ivy League, and while he seems utterly uninterested in the study of modern literature or the writing of poetry—though he has penned three suspense novels—the cultivation of a student like Sarah Elizabeth Pride, who rolls her eyes at Farris's books, seems to underwrite the possibility that this elite network could indeed evolve.

Sarah is a senior with giant eyes and a Celtic poet-nerd fashion sense—she can't hang out with me on a Friday night because a guest speaker is coming to campus to speak Latin, a "nonnegotiable event," which has been in her calendar for weeks. She is your archetypical Patrick Henry overachiever, one of fifty-two students nationwide to receive a fellowship from the Intercollegiate Studies Institute, an organization for the conservative academic elite. Sarah double majors in history and literature, which other top students here say is a near-impossible feat, and has still taken time to be the first woman to run for student body president; she says she didn't expect anyone but a guy to win, but she at least wanted to open up the debate. After she graduates, she hopes to earn a Gates fellowship to study at Cambridge, and plans to return to Patrick Henry as a professor—despite Paul's decree, which she must accept as inerrant according to the statement, "I do not permit a woman to teach or to have authority over a man, but to be in silence."

Even though Sarah has manned polls, phone banked, ridden a bus all the way to Missouri to campaign for Bill Talent, and worked the seventy-hour task force for Bush at the Republican National Committee last year, her true zeal lies in narrative fiction. She has been sketching out an epic novel, a fantasy about a planet parallel to Earth, set two hundred years in the past, that will examine how Jesus Christ's arrival on this planet affected that one. "You know, something Narnia-esque, but fuller. More extensive. Not about homilies but totality. I still have a lot of advanced historical and linguistic research to do before I can sit down to write," she tells me. She sees that while government majors may shape politics, it's literature that changes hearts.

Writing, Sarah has seen firsthand, is an acceptable career for a Christian woman who must also stay at home to raise and school her family. Her mother, Mary Pride, is a chief contributor to a popular homeschooling magazine, and after Christ, her top role model. But Mary Pride was born of a different age to different parents. When she married a nominally but largely nonobservant Christian man, she had no problem with his lack of faith—she was an atheist. As Sarah's dad got older, he became more interested in Christianity, which drove her mother crazy. She thought the intellectual response to his new faith would be to read the Bible even more seriously than he was, so she'd be prepared to challenge him on every theological point.

Gradually, though, Mary Pride began to believe what she was reading, and was eventually born again. She's in the Moses Generation. Mary decided to abandon her secular past. No one ever made her sign a Statement of Faith in her teens or drafted her into a battle she didn't choose on her own as an educated and independent adult. She chose herself to give birth eight times. At age twenty-two she would have never said, as her daughter tells me now, "I've known all my life there is a major battle going on. I've always known it is why we're here as Christians and not instantly raptured away—so we can fight the forces at work."

And so Sarah will keep campaigning. She'll more than likely teach and have many children, and indoctrinate them into what she subscribes to "fully and enthusiastically," since it's all she's ever known. She'll continue to believe that the earth was created in six twenty-four-hour days and that Jesus is coming back to destroy the world and rapture her up to heaven. She'll commit to the inerrancy of a book that compromises her rights. She'll spread the word at phone banks and in novels and magazines. And like every student I meet at Patrick Henry, she will consider herself a first-class intellectual, whom God has personally selected to take back the land.

Sarah's thinking will unfailingly continue to follow two statements Patrick Henry himself made, not nearly as famous as his aphorism "Give me liberty or give me death" but with far greater bearing on the Disciple Generation. The first is explicitly political and intolerant: "It cannot be emphasized too strongly or too often that this great nation was founded not by religionists but by Christians, not on religions, but on the gospel of Jesus Christ!" The second is startlingly anti-intellectual: "The Bible is worth all the other books ever printed." It's a statement I hear paraphrased by young Christians nationwide, and never more than when they speak in defense of creationism.

7

Evolutionary War

What happens when deductive reasoning and the scientific method—or at least its appearance—are embraced by Evangelicals to argue the inarguable? Many believers of inerrancy today are disguised not merely by their tattoos, but often by the mantle of scholarship. When it comes to slicing evolution out of the classroom with Pentecostal zeal, the most active and effective players often reside in the least obvious places. They're neither denizens of the homeschool movement nor do they share a last name with James Dobson, but instead, many are multidegreed apostles whose scholarship is a bait and switch to bolster a creationist agenda. Right now, that agenda is playing out at secular—and even public—schools across the country.

On a warm September evening at George Mason University, Virginia's largest public school, a pickup truck bearing three massive kegs pulls up outside a fraternity house. Nearby, the masthead of *So to Speak*, the campus feminist literary and arts journal, gathers for a meeting. In the economics department, computers hum in the offices of two Nobel laureates. And upstairs from a litter-strewn lounge in the colossal student center, an extracurricular seminar in intelligent design is in full swing. Salvador Cordova, the compact and animated young Philippine American lecturing this evening, writes an equation on a whiteboard, without explaining any of its mysterious variables.

$$\Psi = \Pi\Sigma\Psi O$$

Impressed murmurs issue from the lips of the twenty-five people in the room. "This is what's known as the God equation," Salvador explains to his students, grinning and tapping the whiteboard with a red marker, giddy with "how totally cool it is to have this proof." He fails to mention that it's an equation constructed entirely of variables. Factor zero in for any one of these symbols and you've got what could be known as the atheism equation. Regardless, Salvador continues his lecture. "Theology is truly a branch of physics," he says. "I wanted to cry when I saw this. This theorem proves you can never erase the need for faith."

Salvador is leading the fall semester's first gathering of the George Mason IDEA club, one of the thirty-plus campus chapters of the California-based Intelligent Design and Evolution Awareness Center. Today's participants include a range of undergraduates in computer science, biology, and psychology, in the usual coating of hair gel and self-tanner nineteen-year-olds slather on to impress one another at the beginning of the fall semester. Some enthusiastic paler and older visitors arrive late, among them a middle school science teacher, a high school math teacher, and a campus academic advisor. To accommodate them, a student arranges a second circle of folding chairs around the four packed seminar tables.

A neat, sandy-haired woman wearing a gold cross named Caroline Crocker enters and seats herself in the remaining empty chair, sending whispers of recognition rippling throughout the room. Crocker taught biology at George Mason until her department expressed concerns about her newfound enthusiasm for intelligent design. When she introduces herself, the room explodes with applause. "I was the same as any other scientist," she tells the room, like a recovering addict in group therapy. "I believed what I heard like the rest of them. But I picked up a book on intelligent design five years ago, and it explained to me the things about cell complexity that didn't make sense. It was the science which made me question what I knew. I took some time off and looked into embryology, and I came to the conclusion that we have to consider what we know." Intelligent design is the simple conceit that the world at both its most micro and macro—from the smallest cells to the largest star systems—is so complex that it must have been created by, yes, an intelligent designer. Crocker's words are the wet dream of any promoter of intelligent design: the conversion story spoken in the professional language of science.

The author of the book that made Crocker find a Creator in her petri dish is a leader in the leading organization founded to bring Christian faith into the science classroom. He is one of many scientist-posing activists with an unflinching theist agenda, forcing into science classrooms the idea that the world is too complicated to understand via empirical investigation, so we should stop trying to discover what we don't yet know, and furthermore stop teaching what we do. We should have *faith*, apparently, but not faith in human endeavor or achievements.

While many of the people in this room may tell you that they arrived empirically at their Christian faith, religious conversion is an emotional experience, not an intellectual one. There's no equation of logic (or physics, for that matter) to be applied to faith—that's why it's *faith*. If it made sense it would be called *reason*. The intelligent design movement is faith in reason's clothing—God in a lab coat. These activists translate their stance into the language of the academy, which is, in turn, backed up at the highest levels of our current government.

We don't have to look too far back to find a recent wave of anti-intellectualism recast as enlightenment. Though the New Left kicked off the sixties in an explosion of critical thinking, hedonism quickly subsumed a generation's progress. Drugs obscured what the movement had begun. Hallucinogens promised to open minds, shift perspectives. (Incidentally, Freud said that religious conversion was hallucinatory psychosis.) The sixties *lifestyle* could make you feel like you were part of a movement of intellectuals—or so I've been told—but unless you were shutting down your university, or drafting speeches to be read on the antiwar front lines, your brain was probably just disengaged. Really you were just doing bong hits at a dinner party, or screwing your housemate while tripping your ass off, wondering why his or her face was dripping all over your bean bag chair. Just as the initial core of sixties revolutionaries spawned a population of self-identified intellectuals who were actually just imbibing lifestyle at full force, so this movement decorates its own far scarier pseudointellectualism in the tech-age narcotic of choice: the authority of so-called science.

Before showing a video on intelligent design and cell biology, Salvador reads aloud from a crumpled, yellowed newspaper article, his voice sermonizing while his eyes glow like an excited child's. It's one of his favorite stories, one he referenced three times within the first hour we spoke, about an atheist scientist and professor who became a deist after considering intelligent design. Throughout the evening's session, Salvador tells similar tales of nonbelievers who adopt faith because of their own thinking about science—the atheist astrophysicist who became a believer at fifty—as though they somehow corroborate and lend authority to his own faith. "Most people within the intelligent design movement believe personally that the intelligent designer is God. And for many of us Evangelicals, we follow the Bible first and look to science to confirm its truths," Salvador says, going significantly off-message as a member of a movement that purports interest in nothing but science.

As the most effective proponents of intelligent design would tell you, science, not faith, will open the door to university and high school courses, but science is nowhere to be found in the church proverbs Salvador reads aloud ostensibly to demonstrate "that scientific method points to divine intelligence," or in his lecture on the genealogy of Jesus, which he says proves that "if you go back to the apes, then you're not a Christian." Salvador says he feels called by God to advance the cause of Christianity in the science classroom, but he will not distance himself from his Evangelicalism to do so. That's fine with IDEA's founders—Evangelicals who started the original club out of an evolutionary biology class at UCSD in 1999. The IDEA leadership admits frequently on their Web site that they operate IDEA with a "bias and an agenda" to promote the notion that within intelligent design "the identity of the designer is the God of the Bible."

It's according to this agenda that Salvador founded both this club and one at nearby James Madison University. He's a student at neither school, not that you'd ever know to look at him in his baggy jeans and short sleeves, pulling a textbook-brimming backpack on wheels through campus. Salvador looks twenty, acts thirty, and has amassed an educational and occupational résumé that would be tough to manage by forty. He says he has worked at MIT and the IRS, and holds degrees in computer science, electrical engineering, and mathematics from Virginia Tech and George Mason. A former classical pianist, these days Salvador periodically makes a living as a computer techie, paying the rest of his bills, he confesses to me, by playing blackjack—in fact, he's driving straight from class tonight to a game in upstate New York.

To maintain a gym membership and hold IDEA meetings in the student center Salvador takes an occasional one-hour music class at George Mason; his James Madison connection is through an ex-girlfriend who was a student there. At James

Madison, Salvador commissioned the campus atheist group, the Freethinkers, to poll students about their interest in a class that explores issues of intelligent design and creationism, like one currently taught by a chemistry professor at the University of Minnesota. Of the general student population, 70 percent said they'd like the school to offer such a class, and among biology majors alone, 75 percent expressed interest. Intelligent design proponents now frequently cite the poll, making Salvador one of the movement's most important activists on secular campuses.

Salvador was raised Roman Catholic until high school. He studied evolution in biology class at age sixteen, which did not conflict with his faith, since evolution has long been accepted within the Catholic Church. At age seventeen he was born again while watching Pat Robertson's *700 Club* on late-night television. He immediately felt that one could not believe in a Christian God and also believe in evolution, which, for a math and science kid, was a crisis. "Brute fact epistemology was all I'd ever known," he says. Salvador wrote away for study material prepared by the Institute of Creation Research, which holds as its mission that "only by showing the scientific bankruptcy of evolution, while exalting Christ and the Bible, will Christians be successful in 'the pulling down of strongholds; casting down imaginations, and every high thing that exalteth itself against the knowledge of God, and bringing into captivity every thought to the obedience of Christ' (II Corinthians 10:4, 5)." By the time Salvador enrolled in the engineering program at Virginia Tech, he was an "old earth creationist": he believed each of the days in the Genesis account represents an entire era—what's known as the "day-age" theory.

A few years ago, Salvador experienced an epiphany while he was reading an article about radiometric dating in *Nature*, the science community's journal of record. This article, which discussed the gradual decaying of the speed of light from distant stars, hardly reunited Salvador with Darwin's thinking; instead, by the time he finished reading the article, he had become a "young earth creationist." He thought he'd found proof that the earth was indeed only a few thousand years old, supporting the belief that God created the world literally, as the Bible says, in six days. "The evidence is so clear," he explains to me, tucking into a bloody pile of prime rib at a nearby student haunt before the meeting. "Dinosaurs and men obviously lived at the same time. If the radiometric dating is off, then the geological record doesn't make sense. Rain erodes the landscape, right? So we shouldn't have the fossils we have. They should have been washed away if they're so old."

Soon after Salvador read the *Nature* article, he discovered additional evidence in support of Genesis in a scholarly genetics journal. "I couldn't believe what I was reading—that all women are descended from the same woman. Hello? Mitochondrial Eve? Science proves that you, Lauren, have descended from Eve! And yet even the scientists who prove this refuse to believe!" Salvador's exclamation kicks off a hyperactive monologue that rambles from my personal origins as part of a mythological man's rib to a lecture on protein chemistry, culminating in the following gem: "We could prove Noah's ark through animal DNA but no one is willing to fund it. Where is the commitment to scientific research here?"

Research, though, has little to do with intelligent design. It's an entire theory based on faith and what I call the Whoa Principle. Like, *whoa*, the mathematical probability of the earth's sustainability for humans is stunningly low, or, *whoa*, the level of complexity in a cell is mind-boggling, or in the jargon of the intelligent design movement, is "irreducibly complex." That means it could have never evolved in individual parts: each cell part is required to function in harmony with the other parts, so cells must have been designed this way. *Whoa*, this never could have evolved. It all fairly blows my mind, too.

But there's more to intelligent design than acknowledging the astonishing physical complexity of our world. There's the deep faith that whoever has cooked up our world in some well-equipped heavenly kitchen has done it with a purpose in mind. It's a galling tautology to be passed off as epistemology: our lives have meaning because someone created us to have meaning. In the science talk these folks like to use to make this point, to take an example from a film shown recently at the Smithsonian, the earth is in exactly the perfect place in the arms of the galaxy so we can observe the universe, and the moon is just the right size and distance from the sun so we can see the sun's atmosphere during a solar eclipse. Thus, the argument goes, the Great Architect has created the world for our admiration. "It is the glory of God to conceal a matter, but the glory of kings is to search out a matter, as the heavens for height and the earth for depth," according to Proverbs 25. So long as this is true, we are not alone in an endless and cold and dark universe. So long as this is true, death is not the horrifying utter end of our existence. So long as this is true, there must be someone to watch over me.

The truth that Salvador Cordova, and every intelligent design proponent I have ever known, would like me to accept is not in the end whether a cell's flagellar motor was architected or the earth's gravity was calibrated by an invisible genius—what Salvador would like me to accept is the truth of the Bible. In disseminating that truth, Salvador believes, science and mathematics are the ultimate evangelical tools, the paragon of "sneaky deep." While Salvador cites the Bible more frequently than he does Schrödinger in his lectures, he agrees with the intelligent design movement's strategy to separate scripture from discussions with nonbelievers. "By taking intelligent design away from Christian texts you further the Christian faith," he tells me. "That's how you can reach people who couldn't be reached. That's how you influence the culture, by decoupling the science from the religious text. That's how you change people's metaphysical beliefs."

Secularists may spill a great deal of ink lambasting out-of-the-closet theists encroaching upon our science classrooms, but rarely do they scrutinize what occurs outside known Christian camps. This is where the inroads are plowed. Who isn't impressed by a little math, or by an explanation of something visible only under our most powerful microscopes—especially if you fail to be impressed by the gospel? That's how you open people to what Salvador believes absolutely, that the Bible is the inerrant word of God. It's a strategy based on a classic con move, or the simplest sleight-of-hand trick. Distract your mark with something that both commands his attention and asserts your grasp of something beyond his reach; that's how you open him up for *the get*, by first engaging and then freezing the mind. Salvador knows you can change hearts for Christ the same way.

———

"Today the evolution controversy seems as remote as the Homeric era, to intellectuals in the East," historian Richard Hofstadter wrote in 1962. Hofstadter couldn't have imagined that forty years later—forty years of scientific progress, I should mention—more than three-quarters of American teenagers tell Gallup pollsters they believe their life exists because God created it. Today when intellectuals in the East rustle open their *New York Times*, they are often greeted by a legal struggle to keep religion out of biology classrooms in Kansas or Georgia or Pennsylvania, making the days when these headlines were unthinkable seem as remote as the Homeric era.

Indeed, our current state of affairs would have appeared farcical not just in 1962, but in 1892. Back then, creationism was not a belief of conservative Christians; they embraced *The Origin of the Species* soon after it was published in 1859, guided by evangelist Lyman Beecher, who preached a pro-evolution message nationwide. Creationism raised its head only later, when the popular teachings of Seventh-day Adventist founder Ellen G. White contended that each day cited in

Genesis was a literal twenty-four-hour period. Before White's theology spread, people were quite willing to mesh together new discoveries with the Bible's account, comfortably adapting theology as science advanced.

But as thinkers like Marx and Freud came to redefine personhood as something existing outside biblical concepts, and as the Enlightenment's legacy took root throughout the culture while an intellectual elite developed outside the Christian tradition, resentment and backlash began to percolate. Self-protectionism begat fundamentalism, transforming the Bible from a text of mystery and metaphor to a guidebook whose rule—and inerrancy—was absolute; any challenge to total and abject literalism threatened to crumble its authority. In the Manichaeism that would emerge in the 1920s to define Christianity in America, one was either a Christian soldier battling against amoral science and philosophy or an enemy of the faith: intellectual challenge was tantamount to blasphemy.

Nothing came to represent the threat to the Bible's literal perfection more than evolution. Long after Darwin's ideas had been woven into the public understanding of our origins, the concepts set forth in *The Origin of the Species* were recast as Satanism. William Jennings Bryan became the bullhorn for this mentality, announcing in 1925, "All the ills from which America suffers can be traced back to the teaching of evolution. It would be better to destroy every other book ever written and save just the book of Genesis."

Bryan's one-book philosophy is often called Bible-onlyism. There could be no clearer or more aggressive example of anti-intellectualism; yet often the same people who blame secular mass culture for the downfall of Western civilization are the champions of Bryan's assertion that one needs no book but the Bible. Among the legion young Christians I have known, very few choose to read anything that has not been written explicitly to support the Bible, if in fact they read anything else at all. Self-censorship is inculcated early, infecting the minds of the most urbane and articulate young people with Bryan's thinking.

I recall whiling away a hot afternoon in Council Bluffs, Iowa, sitting on a gritty sidewalk with two extraordinarily witty and thoughtful teenage Extreme Tour musicians, casually wending our way through a conversation about the creative process, the nature of love, family, and friends—just hanging out. One of the guys, a sixteen-year-old with a toppled and faded green mohawk, got to talking about his public high school and how, whether you were a jock or a kid like him, you weren't cool if you weren't Christian. As he picked at the holes in his T-shirt, we talked about how this took the pressure off at parties, and made locker-room disagreements easier to resolve. "When you all believe in basically one right way to live, it frees you up to go about living that way as creatively as possible," he told me. When I asked how this belief system extended beyond the cafeteria and into the science lab, both guys told me without hesitating that their public school taught them creationism, "as backed up by clear scientific proof."

When I challenged them, asserting that perhaps the earth was more than six thousand years old, they shrunk back in horror, lectured me on the fallacy of dinosaurs, carbon dating, distance from the sun, and a host of other explanations one can find on the Internet—and in their classrooms, apparently—and then abruptly ended our conversation. These sharp minds had been coached by their twin towers of institutional influence, illegally in their public high schools and vociferously in their churches, to think that my point of view had the power to destroy all they believed was right. Everything "right" ostensibly supports the idea that, as Patrick Henry College's Statement of Faith says, the Bible is infallible in its entirety; everything else is not just wrong, but evil.

The Reverend D. James Kennedy, the influential founder of the Center for Christian Statesmanship ("Ministering to Those Serving on Capitol Hill") and a leading light of Christian radio and television, told attendees at a Christian conference in 1999: "The Darwinian theory of evolution contradicts not just the book of Genesis, but every word in the Bible from beginning to end." Kennedy's words revive the long-buried ire of late-nineteenth-century evangelist Dwight Moody—as well as his predecessor Patrick Henry—who spouted aphorisms such as, "If there was one portion of the scripture untrue, the whole of it went for nothing," and, "When the word of God says one thing and scholarship says another, scholarship can go to hell!"

In the same conference speech, Reverend Kennedy announced that he was part of a team developing what he called the "wedge strategy," so named because it would drive a wedge into the tree trunk of secular education, toppling Dar-winism in favor of creationism. The wedge strategy is the brainchild of the Discovery Institute, a Seattle-based organization that has emerged as the leader of the intelligent design movement and that continuously asserts in the press that intelligent design has no relationship to faith. In 1999, Discovery drafted a document explaining the wedge strategy for the purpose of attracting funds, which irrefutably exposes the true purpose of the organization's work, revealing that it has as much of a place in science education as the whore of Babylon would in abstinence education. According to the strategy, intelligent design is far more than a concept; it's a Christian battle plan. "Design theory promises to reverse the stifling dominance of the materialist worldview, and to replace it with a science consonant with Christian and theistic convictions," the document says.

The strategy enumerates a list of goals to be achieved within five years, including pushing the evolution debate to the forefront of the press and the national agenda, charting a polling uptake in interest in intelligent design, and seeing ten states begin to push intelligent design in schools. Well before the five-year deadline had arrived, each of Discovery's goals had been surpassed beyond expectation, and as I write, *twenty-two* states are pushing intelligent design in schools. Discovery's twenty-year goals are far more ambitious, but after considering the strategy's short-term effectiveness, perhaps we should regard them as feasible: "to see intelligent design theory as the dominant perspective in science" and "to see design theory permeate our religious, cultural, moral, and political life."

Sloganeering antievolution activists like to say in the

press that their goal with students is merely to "teach the controversy"—an effort to popularly instill the falsehood that evolution is controversial among legitimate scientists and scholars. However, when speaking to a devout audience at his conference, the Reverend Kennedy was comfortable going off-message to explain the wedge strategy in terms of not just faith, but evangelism, echoing Salvador Cordova's avowal that intelligent design is a perfect "sneaky deep" conversion tool. This is the real goal of the movement, he says in no un-certain terms. "The objective is to convince people that Dar-winism is inherently atheistic, thus shifting the debate from creationism versus evolution to the existence of God versus the nonexistence of God. From there people are introduced to the truth of the Bible and then the question of sin and fi-nally introduced to Jesus." The "people" he's talking about are high school and college students: no child left behind.

Key to the wedge strategy is the success of *Darwin's Black Box*, the book that converted Caroline Crocker to her new faith in intelligent design. The book, by Michael Behe, a se-nior fellow at the Discovery Institute and a board member of the IDEA Center, has become the bible of the intelli-gent design movement, selling more than two hundred thousand copies in more than ten languages. Behe is a central-casting-perfect biology professor—spectacles, beard, stooped shoulders—who teaches at Lehigh University. In one of the court cases that claimed prominent space in the *New York Times*, *Kitzmiller v. Dover Area School District*, he was the star witness for the defense.

Eleven parents sued the school board of Dover, Pennsylvania, for requiring, in the spring of 2005, that intelligent design infiltrate biology classes. The trial was a two-month course in the particulars of design theory, played out at the U.S. District Court in Harrisburg, in a federal building constructed during Lyndon Johnson's presidency, when this Scopes-style case was unthinkable. In 1987 the Supreme Court ruled that creationism could not be taught alongside evolution, since it disobeyed the Constitution by advancing a specific faith. With the help of attorneys from the Thomas More Law Center—the ACLU of the religious right—it was up to Behe to prove that intelligent design is not just another term for creationism, or, as he trilled in a constant litany from the witness stand, that it's science and not religion.

The press took notes from seats in the jury box, while pewlike courtroom benches accommodated spectators and local school groups. This must have ranked high on their list of lamest possible field trips; even the judge could barely stay awake during Behe's stultifying testimony, featuring primers on scientific peer review and lecture slides of flagella and blood-clotting cascades. Before the trial, in a *Times* op-ed piece, Behe wrote about the obvious nature of intelligent design: "If it looks, walks, and quacks like a duck, then, absent compelling evidence to the contrary, we have warrant to conclude it's a duck." To apply his logic, since "designer" is simply another word for "creator," we have warrant to conclude that design theory quacks like creationism because it is one and the same.

The *Kitzmiller* case directed a national spotlight onto the small town of Dover, just a short drive south of Harrisburg. Dover is a cluster of shabby Victorian homes, pizza parlors, and beauty salons set amid the farms that provide most of the area's decaying livelihood. Near the center of town, down the block from a church whose sign encourages parishioners, BE AN ORGAN DONOR—GIVE YOUR HEART TO JESUS, is a low brick high school. Outside the building, kids smoke and swear; they bitch about getting grounded and discuss whose house can host their narcotic indiscretions after school. Inside the building, on a shelf in the library, are fifty-odd donated copies of a textbook called *Of Pandas and People*.

Just as George Hunter's *Civic Biology* textbook landed John T. Scopes in a Tennessee courtroom eighty years ago, *Of Pandas and People*, written in part by Behe, was key to the case in Pennsylvania. *Pandas* explains that "various forms of life began abruptly with distinguishing features already intact: fish with fins and scales, birds with feathers, beaks, and wings, etc.," paraphrasing the Genesis account of life's origins. The Texas-based Foundation for Truth and Ethics, a conservative Christian think tank with connections to the Discovery Institute, originally published the textbook to teach creationism, but after the 1987 Supreme Court ruling, the foundation swapped the term "creationism" for "intelligent design."

As a result of the Dover school board's decision to be the first in the nation to mandate a reference to intelligent design in biology classrooms, teachers were ordered to read a four-paragraph statement to students, suggesting design as an alternative to evolution. The board required them to point students to further study in *Pandas*, copies of which were mysteriously placed in science classrooms after the decision.

While the case in Harrisburg—and the rest of the national legal debate—hinged on the defense's ability to prove that religion has nothing to do with design, everyone in Dover recognized the Christian impetus behind the school board's actions. The whole town knew about board members' proselytizing and telling nonbelievers they were doomed to Hell, and they'd all heard about the board member who stood up at a meeting and bellowed, "Two thousand years ago someone died on a cross. Isn't someone going to take a stand for him?"—stories that alarmed enough voters to replace the entire school board on election day.

Two months after Behe's testimony, presiding judge John E. Jones released a 139-page decision. He ruled that intelligent design is religion in sheep's clothing; it must be barred from the science classroom because it violates the establishment clause. Jones wrote in his conclusion, "This case came to us as the result of the activism of an ill-informed faction on a school board, aided by a national public interest law firm eager to find a constitutional test case on ID, who in combination drove the board to adopt an imprudent and ultimately unconstitutional policy. The breathtaking inanity of the board's decision is evident when considered against the factual backdrop which has now been fully revealed through this trial." In other words, he regarded the actions of the Dover school board—in congress with the agenda-driven Thomas More Law Center—to be a flawed but clear creationist strategy. He went on to deride the defendants in no uncertain words: "It is ironic that several of these individuals, who so staunchly and proudly touted their religious convictions in public, would time and again lie to cover their tracks and disguise the real purpose behind the ID Policy."

Upon hearing the news that this self-described conservative, religious, and even *Republican* judge exposed the truth of intelligent design, euphoric secularists filled the nations' editorial pages with smug approval. Their foes cried foul: John West, a senior fellow at the Discovery Institute, wrote on the institute's Web site that the decision is "judicial activism with a vengeance," and that Jones's ruling was motivated by careerism, because "he wanted his place in judicial history." What West did not write was that every time a judicial door slams shut, the movement redoubles its strength through outrage and a renewed sense of urgency.

Moreover, intelligent design proponents keep quiet about the idea that Jones's decision opens new legal support to teach their views in philosophy and religion classes. "We do not question that many of the leading advocates of ID have bona fide and deeply held beliefs which drive their scholarly endeavors. Nor do we controvert that ID should continue to be studied, debated, and discussed. As stated, our conclusion today is that it is unconstitutional to teach ID as an alternative to evolution in a public school science classroom," Jones wrote, suggesting that intelligent design is a legitimate field of study outside biology class. This is a victory to an intelligent design movement that thinks in small steps, always taking the long view; any opportunity to introduce theism in the classroom is a push forward.

To be sure, a legal victory would have been a boon to the movement, but no intelligent design group worth its salt supports Dover's attention-getting bid for influence in the science classroom. Even the most brazen creationist groups, like Answers in Genesis—the name says it all—don't approve of requiring teachers to deride evolution or direct students to *Pandas*, since that's just courting a lawsuit, and likely an unwinnable one. Lawsuits, even the Rock for Life kids would tell you, aren't the way to change hearts and minds. Most groups agree that the best way to convert a generation to the concept of intelligent design is to use stealth: hire Evangelical teachers in mainly Christian communities, and make sure the local church elders have a presence on the PTA. This is exactly what is happening all over the country, beyond the gaze of newspaper assignment editors and pro bono prosecutors, and it's working.

THE FEAR OF THE LORD IS THE BEGINNING OF KNOWLEDGE, says a sign at the entrance of the Christian School of York, a private Christian academy a few miles from Dover High School that, little by little, public schools have begun to resemble.

The daily devotionals in homeroom earlier this morning were spoken with a little extra passion to support the Lady Crusaders, the girls' volleyball team, in their tournament tonight. In the science lab, half the students wear tie-dyed "Crusader" T-shirts to encourage the squad. But Leslie Hardeman, a blond senior who is one of the team's star players, isn't thinking about volleyball—she's outraged about the Dover case.

"The work of the Creator on trial? Yeah, right. Could it be any more ridiculous? Take the bats who give off sonar to find their food and who use it as a natural defense," she says. (*Whoa.*) "Evolutionists would be, like—what's that called?"

A teammate chirps, "Adaptation?"

"Yeah. Adaptation. Whatever," she scoffs. "I mean, no matter how you look at it, the truth is God created it that way to protect the species. There's no way that could have evolved."

Her teammate pipes up again. "Seriously. Think about our brains. It's just a lump of stuff, and yet it makes us feel!" (*Whoa.*)

"Right? It's ludicrous. It takes more faith to believe in evolution than to believe there's a Creator."

Twenty-five-year-old biology teacher Andrew Nagle listens proudly to this exchange. He, after all, taught these students about life's origins directly from the Bible, which he is permitted to do because his school is private and thus beyond the scope of state court rulings. He begins his course with Genesis I and II, "our fundamental starting point for biology," he explains to me between classes, which he follows up with some course work about cells, and then a little bit of chemistry, after which the class discusses "the complexity of life" according to *Darwin's Black Box*. In February, Andrew's students formally debate creationism versus evolution. "Who do *you* think always wins?" he snickers, setting his Bible on top of the bio textbook at the front of the room. Scripture finds its way into every class taught here, in the curriculum and the surroundings; on the lab bookshelf is a weathered copy of *The Christian View of Science and Scripture*; a flag bearing a golden cross hangs over the blackboard.

Since today's homeroom devotionals were so intense, Andrew skips the usual prayer to open physics class, opting instead to share a little general wisdom. "Atheists in universities are all in the philosophy department now," he instructs his seniors. "No one is left in the science departments. You'll see next year in college. Physics is a methodology for understanding created order. Systems reflect back to a Creator. So let's keep that in mind." Realizing this material is a little dry for this crowd just several years his younger, Andrew runs a hand through his spiky brown hair and shifts tack to tell a story about the "awesome" time he had making a pipe bomb out of a potato at Grove City College four years ago. "It was totally sick, man," he tells the class, a grin illuminating his round face.

During Andrew's senior year at a nearby public high school, he wrote the names of several Christian colleges in a circle and spun a stick to see where it pointed; when it landed on Grove City College, he figured his enrollment there was preordained. Now, in the midst of his third year teaching science, computers, and the Bible at the Christian School, he's the cool teacher on campus. In class, Andrew brags about scoring tickets to a Christian rock festival; he knows all the gossip on campus; even his female students confide in him about their allegedly chaste boyfriends. Last year he made a music video, a rather funny and accurate imitation of Eminem's *Lose Yourself*—his was called *Quiz Yourself*—to teach eight central principles of biology. In his video, Andrew pulls a hooded sweatshirt low over his face and raps:

First evolution, Chuckie D's flawed solution
Atheism endowed, the whole crowd goes so loud

The tough topics, catastrophic—wazzup bioethics?
Human life's value? Uh oh, things are getting hectic!
All the pain inside amplified by the fact
That scientists try to provide
And even undermine the meaning of life, hedonism justified

These are concepts Andrew learned not just in Christian college, but at the public school he attended near Harrisburg, where every high school administrator was Evangelical, and allowed what Andrew calls "more Christianized opportunities than were legally permitted." What he means is that his teachers maligned evolution and taught Bible-based creationism. This is hardly a local aberration; I've met many people across the country who have been taught the Genesis account at public schools, like those Extreme Tour kids who attend high school in the South and the Midwest. Watching Andrew in front of his class, it occurs to me that I am watching the first-generation result of what happens when evolution is not taught in schools: graduates hone and perpetuate a cycle. "The cool thing about teaching at the school," he whispers to me conspiratorially, "is I basically *am* the curriculum here."

At the Christian School of York, Andrew does what his teachers before him did, but in the idiom of the movement, putting to use that cool-kid, rock-'n'-roll, relational-evangelism twist. Teaching in generational vernacular, he follows his biology textbook except where origins are concerned, which he thinks is exactly what biologists would want him to do. "We didn't understand intelligent design a hundred years ago because we didn't have the right microscopes to see the complexity of cells, we didn't have the right thinking. And the people who write bio textbooks know this," he explains to me one afternoon in the computer lab. "But rather than deal with the earth-shattering implications intelligent design poses for Western society, they say, 'We may as well keep living the lie.' "

Andrew, like Salvador Cordova, is convinced the earth is only several thousand years old. "Archaeologists know carbon dating is a joke," he says. "God created the earth to look old to test our faith. True science doesn't disagree with what the Bible says. If the Bible is truth, then science coincides." Any science that disagrees with the Bible, he believes, threatens the very existence of God, and such science exists, he says, only "because people want to cling to justifications to satisfy themselves. Without God there's nothing stopping me from doing whatever I want. Evolution justifies hedonism and relativity," or so he teaches his students.

In biology class one morning, a senior in a white polo shirt, who leads the school in both good grades and amassing girls' crushes, draws a cell on the blackboard and explains its different parts to the class. "Looks pretty irreducibly complex, right?" he says. After class we talk about how he has been influenced by his teacher—he has even applied early decision to Andrew's alma mater—and by what he has learned in class. He tells me that the class, as well as *Darwin's Black Box*, of which he speaks with reverence, taught him not only about the falsehood of evolution, but about the truth of God's existence. "It's all helped me to defend scientifically why I believe in a Creator, and why there's no gray area here," he says between Behe-esque flagellum references.

There's another book that has influenced him, which Andrew assigns every year in the Bible class he also teaches in the science lab. "Everything around you—all of creation—exists because *'God said it.'* He spoke it all into creation," the book says. "It is only in God that we discover our origin, our identity, our meaning, our purpose, our significance, and our destiny." Many more people than the hundreds Andrew will teach, or the hundreds of thousands who will read Behe's book, have absorbed this lesson and repeated it like a mantra. In fact, 20 million people have in the past few years alone committed themselves to these words. It's not a lesson from scripture, but from the best-selling nonfiction book of all time: Rick Warren's self-help bible, *The Purpose-Driven Life*.

In 1969, Thomas Harris's *I'm OK, You're OK* blew open the self-help market, paving the way for Warren's sensation. Even if people that year were chemically detaching their brains from their own wartime realities, at least they still read literature—*Portnoy's Complaint*, and not Harris's consoling hardback, was the best-selling book of the year. Self-help then was no more the province of high school classrooms than creationism was, and the notion that teachers would assign a book that would tell kids, *If you have secular friends, they're going to hell and it's* your *fault*, would have been the imagined product of a bad trip.

Many kids have told me they are "taught" *The Purpose-Driven Life* in public classrooms—under the radar, of course. It's not just Christian schools that are instructing students to memorize Warren's "inspirational" aphorisms, like this commandment of abject anti-intellectualism: "The Bible must always have the first and last word in my life." These kids are learning *in school* that their life's goal is to fulfill the Lord's commission to convert as many souls as possible to bring about "history's conclusion." I suppose when you abandon faith in science, the impending end of the world is a lot easier to accept as truth. After all, it's in the Bible.

8

The Last Generation

_____

On a Sunday at New Life Church in Colorado Springs, I see the following event repeated at every service held in the megachurch's main sanctuary.

"How many of you think we're living in the last days?" the guest pastor, in a slick suit and expensive shaggy haircut, barks at the seventy-five hundred congregants in the cavernous room.

All present raise their hands.

"That's right! You got to be blind not to see we're living in the last days."

"_Amen!_"

"How many of you know we're in a war?"

All present raise their hands again.

"That's right! This is not a playground but a battleground."

"_Amen!_"

New Life's three worship spaces and its World Prayer Center stand like an annex to the Air Force Academy just across Highway 27. The church campus exterior is shrouded in the air force colors of silver and blue, its giant sanctuary like a mother ship to the academy chapel, whose nave rises like a row of bayonets piercing the sky. Three quarters of air force cadets self-identify as Evangelical and 90 percent are Christian; one quarter of all cadets call New Life their home church. These battle-fit young men spend their Friday and Saturday nights worshiping with youth pastors or hanging out at the 24/7 Missions café in the main building, milling around a hulking statue of an angel called *The Exalter*. Forget your notion of harp-wielding cherubim: at New Life an angel is all bronze brawn and veiny sinew, taught and bulging muscles brandishing a mammoth sword, ready for combat. This is drop-and-give-me-twenty Christianity.

These Christian soldiers are no tired metaphor; the God they serve may be intangible, but their guns and ammo are as real as the war they're fighting in the Middle East. Throughout the rest of the Disciple Generation, when people talk about war, they're referring to a domestic us-against-them struggle between secular and Christian Americans, à la Teen Mania's Ron Luce; outside of this largely military town, I have almost never heard Iraq mentioned. In Colorado Springs, our domestic religious struggle and the conflict in Iraq simply represent different theaters in the same holy war. Focus on the Family functions as a military training base here, just like Peterson AFB across the highway.

One morning I meet Greg Martin, a rangy twenty-nine-year-old academy instructor accompanied by his very blond wife, for a cup of 24/7 Missions coffee and a chat about the war. The Martins wear matching red sweaters and talk angrily about Christian persecution around the world, often finishing each other's sentences. "Are we in that region because of God's calling on our country? Absolutely. Christ said if you're not for me you're against me," Greg tells me. He says he knows that "the time of struggle" is nearing an end, and that his cadets are part of the plan to usher in the end of days on the Arabian peninsula. "There's a calling on my generation to be there. We're the ones who can fulfill the Great Commission," he says.

The Great Commission is the biblical requirement that every tongue and tribe on earth must speak Jesus' name before he returns; it's the reason why the Martins and their entire Christian military world believe we are at war in Iraq. "God is saying, 'Onward, Christian soldiers,' even if the government isn't allowed to," Greg calmly lectures me. The rest of the Disciple Generation may intend to end secular life as we nonbelieving Americans know it, but the military arm of the movement has much broader designs: these amassing troops aim to convert every nation.

The airmen of New Life Church avow without equivocation that it's their calling to deliver the Second Coming. God has selected the U.S. military as the vehicle to bring about the end times, they tell me. This is more than a cursory assignment: they're in it to win it. While it's up for debate whether God's on their side, there's no doubt that their Evangelical commander in chief—and his national security advisor—leads their ranks.

The militant urgency of the last days is a great conversion tool, offering purpose to lives lacking focus. Participating in the end distracts from the pain and chaos of this life.

One soldier told me it got him over a car accident that killed his girlfriend when he was at the wheel—"What will it matter when the earth is no more?" Taking up arms in the name of the Lord imbues these true believers with a profound sense of importance, a crucial identity, and a clear sense of meaning in their lives. This Rambo-apostle image of themselves forgives their own deeds on the battlefield, justifying bloodshed as necessary to fulfill the Bible's mission in a holy war. Just as the Extreme Tour's skaters are called to save at-risk kids, Mars Hill's members are called to save Seattle, and Rock for Life's activists are called to save the unborn, the parishioners of New Life Church are called to save the world—so they can end it.

Pastor Ted Haggard grew this megachurch from a congregation of three people perched on lawn chairs in his basement. Today, New Life is just a fraction of his spiritual empire: in addition to leading his colossal church, he heads up the 30 million members of the National Association of Evangelicals. Haggard cuts an appealing figure, with crinkly eyes, a gleaming white smile, and a preference for denim shirts to dark suits, which give him the appearance of a supporting character in *Giant*, a chatty ranch hand with a heart of gold. He believes not just that God has given Christians dominion over the earth but that, as I have heard him declare triumphantly, "the strongest military in the world is opening the door to your ministry. The Islamic people are enraged for a reason—because the Christians are moving in on them." The rhetoric sounds like vintage Bush, but Haggard likely deserves some credit for the president's holy-war speak; every Monday he has a standing phone call with the Oval Office.

When Haggard considers the culture and commerce of

our world, he sees strong parallels to the era in which Jesus was born, and views those parallels as God's preparation for the Second Coming. Today, he points out, the United States plays the same superpower role as Rome; the gospel disseminates in the dominant language of English just as it spread in Greek; and Christianity flows through our global marketplace as it did down newly opened trade routes in biblical times. These elements exist purely for effective evangelism, he contends, part of how "God has supernaturally prepared this generation." Globalism is especially key: he explains the WTO demonstrations as explicitly anti-Christian, protesting not trade but evangelism throughout the world.

"This generation is the first that is capable of actually fulfilling the Great Commission," Haggard believes. Every twenty-four hours, he says, 69,000 new Christians convert, Pentecostal churches hold 30,000 baptisms, and Christians distribute 170,000 copies of the Bible and 11 million scripture portions throughout the world. And each day, he declares, American soldiers make it safe for people to go to church in the Middle East.

Among Haggard's congregants is Gordon Harrell, a ruddy-faced first lieutenant who hails originally from Las Vegas. Gordon's ginger crew cut is shorn on the side and spiked on top with gel that resists the weight of his green battle helmet. His intense gray eyes shine beneath a low brow, and, at thirty-two, his chin has begun to sag. Gordon drives a giant black Ford 150 and reads a giant black edition of the Open Bible. As Haggard once did, Gordon gathers people weekly for prayer in his basement. He, too, prepares sermons, but not for New Life; Gordon's sermons are to share with Sunnis, Shias, and American soldiers in Iraq, where he'll fight this winter. While he awaits deployment, he leads one New Life cell group called A Hunger for God at the Peterson Air Force Base, another called Doing Life Together that convenes to play paintball after Sunday morning worship, and a Bible study in his home.

In a brand-new subdivision down the road from the church, Gordon lives with his roommate, Tim, a freckled guy in his early twenties who, when I first ask his age, smirks and tells me, "Just a few years old as a Christian." Gordon marches around the house with the command of a disciplinarian father while Tim plays the younger clown in sweat socks. When contractors were building the house a few months ago, Gordon brought teams of men inside the raw structure to pray over the house and to cover every inch of timber in Bible verses written in Sharpies and ballpoint pens. Upstairs, these scrawls are buried under a stretch of drywall decorated with a framed cross bearing the words THE FULL ARMOR OF GOD; beside it hang camouflage jackets and helmets on coat hooks. In the basement, the exposed beams and the underside of the staircase are mottled black and blue with scripture, every word aggressively inked in the awkward penmanship of young men.

Gordon lights vanilla candles in his basement sanctuary, as members of the Bible study gather in a circle of lawn chairs and couches, jammed between a foosball table and a laundry machine. Tim strums an acoustic guitar and leads the group—five men representing the air force and the army, as well as a couple of "girlfriends"—in a few unembarrassed worship songs. After singing, the group sits silently with closed eyes and bowed heads while Gordon whispers prayers, his lips moving quickly, candlelight flickering off the silver edges of the Bible pages resting in his lap. Once he finishes his prayer, a jet overhead rips through the silence. Gordon clears his throat and asks Senior Master Sergeant Wayne Babb, a willowy, caramel-skinned Trinidadian from the Bronx, to read aloud the first portion of the day's study. Wayne unzips his camouflage Bible cover, runs a hand over his tight black peak of hair, and recites Revelation 4: " 'The four living creatures, each having six wings, were full of eyes around and within. And they do not rest day or night, saying: "Holy, holy, holy, Lord God Almighty, who was and is and is to come." ' "

Tim exhales deeply during the reading, his excitement uncontainable. "I can't wait to see those creatures covered with eyes. They're doing what we will do. We'll never eat, we'll never sleep, and we'll just worship God all the time. I can't wait for this to finally happen, to see this when the end comes."

Gordon asks, "Who will actually be around for the Tribulation? Will it be us as the Body of Christ? Will we be the only ones resurrected?"

Wayne answers with confidence. "It will also be the 144,000 people coming out of Israel who the Bible says will have to accept Christ before he comes back. I think it's gonna be all young men. I heard that on a TBN show a pastor had teaching on Bible prophecy. I heard they were all alive today."

A former army soldier bows his gleaming shaved head over an enormous Bible and continues the reading, solemnly interjecting verses from different translations—"for accuracy"—of the Lamb with seven horns and seven eyes: " 'You are worthy to take the scroll, and open its seals; for you were slain, and have redeemed us to God by your blood out of every tribe and tongue and people and nation, and have made us kings and priests to our God; and we shall reign on earth.' "

Tim trembles, hugging his guitar tight against his rugby shirt. "It's coming. It's actually coming."

"I think anytime we have doubt in our hearts we should read this chapter," Gordon tells the group. "This was the beginning of the Great Commission. John saw there was so much work that needed to be done, all these people who still haven't been saved. We're gonna see that moment when Jesus Christ opens up the scroll and our names are gonna be on it. It's encouraging."

"Does this mean *we* will reign on earth?" asks one of the girlfriends, her sunburned pink face wide with wonder.

Gordon nods solemnly.

"First Thessalonians says all the Christians who have died will rise from the graves and then those who remain on earth will be caught up in the clouds," explains the army soldier. "The trumpet will sound and we'll be gone. And then this world is gonna be gone. He's gonna destroy earth. Nothing here will matter. The demons will profess his name. Every knee will bow. There will be a day."

"It's coming. It's actually coming," Tim says again.

"If you look at history, nothing comes close except these

times," Gordon murmurs softly. "Look at the whole globe. In the Mideast. In Iraq. The world is preparing for what's gonna happen. If you're not preaching the end right now, you need to be. We are the ones who will make this happen."

"When young people come into the air force we need to try to get to them," says Wayne with a combatant's determination.

Gordon nods again. "I didn't seek the Lord until I was in the military," he says.

Every Friday night at New Life is a service called the Mill, where more than one thousand twenty-somethings meet to worship in a sanctuary designed to look like a bunker. The huge rectangular space is painted to suggest giant cinder blocks, while bare steel joists loom high over the congregation. Gordon ushers a new cadet through one of the many sets of double doors into the hall, where the drummer in the worship band is pounding the skins fast and loud. As the beat crescendoes, the crowd writhes ecstatic, palms are offered to the sky, eyes squeeze shut, and faces tilt toward the battle drums, lit red from spotlights above. As sparse guitars begin to cry out, machines onstage discharge smoke, a gray fog that slowly envelops the young mass that crowds the pulpit. The rest of the band joins in, their rhythmic, steady-beating din drawing callisthenic jumping from the troops, the smell of sweat gradually overwhelming the ashy scent from the smoke hanging in the air. As Gordon's cadet nervously surveys the activity, lyrics are projected on giant screens that bracket the stage, and the crowd begins to sing: *Freedom is ours, We take it* up / *Jesus makes us a free generation / Spreading salvation, Freedom for the world.*"

Listening to the lyrics, Gordon shoots me a smile: the day before, he suggested to me that I title this book *The Freedom Generation*. A young pastor takes the stage and instructs the congregation to lay their hands over their hearts and pray for "the liberty in Christ." It's as though they are pledging allegiance to the flag for their religious salvation, which, to many here, is exactly what's happening—as at Patrick Henry College, it's the flag, not the cross, that graces this space. Christianity, in this generation, is interchangeable with nationalism. During the service, the pastor and worship leader mention freedom more than thirty times; Bush's speechwriters—or Ted Haggard—couldn't have scripted this better if they tried.

A slightly older crowd gathers for Saturday night, the hellfire VH1 equivalent to the Mill's nationalist MTV. Gordon hunkers down near the back while Wayne jumps along to the worship band near the stage, his body lithe and springy, while his hands pump the air above his head. When men gather in the front to lay hands on a congregant about to go out on the mission field, Wayne's arms stretch toward the young evangelist, taut and extended in blessing; during the sermon on hell his fingers clench in tight knots.

"We're preaching fire and brimstone tonight!" the pastor cries breathlessly. His sermon enumerates the specific physical attributes of the afterlife for unrepentant heathens like me, floridly conjuring levels of pain and suffering that make what these soldiers have survived in the Middle East seem like a year on leave. At New Life, even a message about eternally burning flesh ends in an ode to a militaristic apocalypse. "The Bible says one day every knee will bend and every tongue will speak, 'Christ is Lord.' Every defeated army will be in subjugation. They're gonna know," declares the pastor to a whooping and cheering audience. He closes the service in a responsive prayer to remind these enlisted men of their larger mission, his clear, young voice leading the substantial throng.

"Through Christ I am victor."

"Through Christ I am victor."

"You have given me the power to rescue people."

"You have given me the power to rescue people."

"You have filled me with power."

"You have filled me with power."

"You have called me with purpose."

"You have called me with purpose."

"You have made me an agent of your kingdom."

"You have made me an agent of your kingdom."

"Amen."

"Amen."

And the crowd goes wild.

After Wayne and Gordon catch their breath, we head out for a late supper at California Pizza Kitchen with other members of their "focus group," which meets weekly to discuss direction for military ministry. Gordon talks about the sermons he is writing to preach to Iraqis. "They need to hear what freedom is—serving Jesus is freedom," he says, ripping into his pizza. "God's purpose in having troops in Iraq is to give them an opportunity to hear his message." Gordon believes his Lord has called him into the air force specifically to minister in Iraq. He comments frequently that God is using the United States military as his tool, and that he has strategically placed a major military presence where salvation is most needed. This God does, he says, with a single, explicit purpose—to achieve the Great Commission and bring Jesus back to earth.

More than anyone Gordon knows at New Life, Wayne has seen firsthand the work done by combat boots on the ground, having only recently returned from ten years overseas. He, too, believes that his work as a soldier is merely camouflaged work as a missionary. "If you're a Christian, being in the military is the best way to be on the mission field," Wayne says, smiling at his good fortune. "We're out there on the U.S. government dime. They house you, feed you, and pay you to be missionaries on the front line. We all know that's what we're there for. We all know what's behind this war."

———

The conceit that we are living in the last days is hardly unique to the New Life zip code. Since the first century A.D., believers have averred the end is nigh, but never before have Evangelicals dominated the military, or shaped wars from behind the desk of the world's last remaining superpower. Mass culture propagates end-times paranoia on apocalyptic Christian talk shows, and through a vast library of eschatological literature that ranges from self-published tracts to the 40 million published copies of the Left Behind books, not to mention its namesake video game (designed by a born-again Jew who attempted to convert me through recitations of Hebrew astrology).

I can't help but wonder how many of Wayne and Gordon's charges read the Left Behind series and signed up for the air force after imagining themselves as rakish pilot Rayford Steele, but instead of being left on earth like the protagonist of this cautionary tale, dreamed of their own rapture. Likewise, our president seems to be playacting *Left Behind*'s Steele at the helm of the Tribulation Force—"Mission Accomplished," indeed. Even Rick Warren's self-help book lends its soothing voice to the end-times craze, instructing *Purpose-Driven* readers to scrutinize current events for signs of the apocalypse with "Great Commission eyes." But these days, one doesn't need a mental revelation filter to interpret the news—not since the White House offered one of its two hundred coveted press passes to William Koenig, director of Koenig's International News, a Christian prophecy organization that focuses its "news coverage" on the biblical consequences of dividing Israel.

The end of days is hardly just fodder for best-selling writers, bogus news organizations, and conspiracy geeks, now that some Christian academic circles have begun to treat the apocalypse with scholarly urgency. While few accredited institutions feature the Second Coming in their course catalogs, some minor think tanks and marginalized centers of higher learning are applying Revelation's bearing on current (and future) events to their studies. One leading scholar is Robert Livingston, a writer and researcher in upstate New York, who has written a book called *Christianity and Islam:*

The Final Clash. Livingston is unexpectedly tweedy and soft-spoken for someone who has chosen roaring end-times hell-fire as his obsession; his "Great Commission eyes" are the equivalent of horn-rimmed spectacles.

When Livingston discovered Bible prophecy fifteen years ago, his response was to become a missionary. Ten years ago, while on a mission in Turkey, he began to look deeply into eschatology with an eye toward the Islamic world and saw parallels between the methods and agenda of jihadists and what was laid out in the book of Revelation. Like the folks in Colorado Springs, Livingston believes God is using the U.S. military to bring back Jesus Christ and to lay the groundwork to fight the Antichrist—the Beast, as he is called in the Bible. "Is it possible an Islamic jihad will install the Beast at the head of a conquered state?" he wonders in his book. "Perhaps he'll rise up in Iraq, the heart of old Babylon and the mouth of the kingdom of the Beast who is coming." Livingston suggests that if your money is on Pope Benedict for the Antichrist, you should switch your odds to Moqtada al-Sadr—there's a reason, he says, that God has sent us to fight them.

Every conflict has worked to further the Great Commission, Livingston says. Communism, which eschatologists long flagged as the Antichrist's movement, not only opened the door for the Moral Majority's opposing influence but for renewed Christianity—Livingston glories in asserting that communism in Russia crumpled finally on Christmas Day. In the former Yugoslavia, war advanced the gospel, he tells me, when Christians flooded the region to establish churches in its aftermath. "Whenever the U.N. says, 'Help,' in come the

Christian NGOs, and we get closer to the end," he leans forward to tell me in a soft but foreboding voice. "The midst of chaos is always opportunity for the gospel." This has never been truer than in Iraq, where forty Evangelical churches have been planted since Baghdad fell under the firepower of American troops. "He's gonna wrap this thing up soon," says Livingston. *Soon?* I ask him. *Like, fifty years?* "I'd be shocked if it took that long. Based on my research we're looking at ten to thirty years tops." He studies my face for a beat and takes a deep breath. "Seriously," he says. "You are a part of the last generation."

Livingston tracks the progress of the Great Commission on a database run by the missions group Operation Mobilization. When Jesus said every nation must speak his name, he wasn't referring to geopolitical nations, Livingston explains, but distinct "people groups," of which there are sixteen thousand in the world. Thirty years ago missionaries had reached less than half of these people groups, but today less than 2 percent are completely unreached, and less than 30 percent have what missionaries consider an insignificant number of believers. On the Operation Mobilization list are unsaved tribes of Chinese and Turks residing smack in the middle of various possible military conflicts, supporting Livingston's allegation that God uses war to convert unbelievers.

In these penultimate days, many mission groups have jettisoned the notion of building houses and feeding the poor in countries with a strong Christian presence—which, we now know from the database, crosses off 70 percent of the world—and are strategically targeting the not-yet-converted.

They've got an apocalypse to attend to, which can color a man's worldview. "The realization that Jesus is coming balances our sense of God—how we see all the chaos and suffering in the world," Livingston tells me, his voice tight with sincerity. "When kids get molested, well, that just motivates me to get Jesus Christ back here quicker." I think I see a tear welling up in his eye, which I bet is not for those usefully molested kids, but because he believes he's rushing my own hideous demise.

You think life is tough now? Just wait until the Great Commission is completed. Here's how Livingston sees the Bible's science-fiction epilogue coming to light. For example, picking up where we left off at Gordon's Bible study, there is the ride of the Four Horsemen of the Apocalypse. First, red horses ride, which Livingston interprets as a jihadist world war; then come the black horses in the form of economic disaster; next, with the ride of the white horses, the Beast conquers all wealthy nations. Then Babylon is destroyed, which seems to bring the Iraq crisis full circle, right? Wrong. Livingston devotes an entire chapter of his book to why my beloved city, New York, is actually Babylon. She "serves the God of Wealth!" She is a "City of Luxury and Greed!" She "has a Female Idol on a Pedestal!" She will be "Obliterated by Nuclear Attack!" This preview, by the way, counts for just one verse from a single chapter in the entire book of Revelation.

For those of you on the West Coast, it's not any better: I sat down recently with another professorial doomsayer, a white-haired and wild-eyed geologist who points out that

Hollywood is on a fault line, and that we can trace the march to the Second Coming in the movement of the earth's tectonic plates. This is a woman who charts the rapid ascent of the Beast through the recent hurricanes that have ravaged the American South, and who gleefully imagines the Asian tsunami as a precursor to her own rapture. Apparently we unbelievers will see tidal waves roll up the mountains, annihilating everything in their paths. For those of us who won't be marching lockstep behind Gordon and Wayne into the heavenly arms of some eye-covered creature, it only gets much, much worse from there. What person who feels that tiny paranoid tickle, nagging, *What if they're right?* would choose to be left behind? Perhaps nothing motivates conversion more than fear.

An Episcopal priest in Colorado Springs calls the book of Revelation a book of hate within a book of love. He prefers not to teach Jesus as a fire-breathing fascist, nor does he suggest that his God is a God who would torture and smite every being that did not fall to its knees and beg for mercy in his name. Other members of mainline churches have told me the same thing: Revelation was the apostle John's nightmare, or a drug-induced hallucination, or was written by the pen of runaway hubris or insecure wrath. But every day members flee mainline congregations, rejecting churches that suggest an intellectual engagement with scripture, preferring instead the comfort of Evangelical folds that demand conformity to biblical inerrancy. If the Good Book says the creatures will be covered in eyes, then, by God, they will be, and if it says this world will cease to exist once every tribe knows Christ is

Lord, then, as my grandmother once cried out when a plane carrying my family suddenly dropped hundreds of feet, *this is it, kids.*

If you're staring down the end of days, convinced you are a member of the last generation on earth, chances are this line of thinking will lead your perspective on the world. It will more than likely affect how you consider the importance of global warming, or the state of public education, or the proliferation of homeless and hungry Americans. It's sure to direct your thinking about foreign policy, especially in the Middle East; you'll probably consider candidates on a ballot with "Great Commission eyes."

And so the lessons of the sixty-five preceding books of the Bible slide away. Forget all that business about caring for the needy, all of those exhortations for righteousness and humility, that pesky Golden Rule. What's even the point of the meek inheriting the earth if there will be no more earth to inherit? If salvation through heartfelt belief, not acts benefiting others, will ensure your rapture before the Tribulation begins, what's the point of social welfare? Why grieve for the bloody Muslim bodies that pile higher every day? Instead, believers grieve for the unreached in their own lives: Judy Abolafya at Mars Hill grieves for her mother; Samantha Hammer in Rock for Life grieves for her boyfriend; Gordon Haller grieves for me. "God holds you responsible for the unbelievers who live around you," Rick Warren writes. "If you are part of God's family, your mission is mandatory."

When I was traveling with the Extreme Tour, I asked Ted Bruun how he knew absolutely that all this was real. He looked me square in the eye and smiled warmly. "How do you know you love your husband?" he asked in return. "But you know, right? You are as sure of that love—of the truth of that love—as you are that you are alive. And you're motivated by that love, right? It's the same thing." That parallel I could recognize. His impetus to evangelize was rooted in a sense of genuine accountability to others; his urge to reach out to strangers motivated by a genuine fear that we will be left behind.

After wrapping up the evening's Bible study in his basement, Gordon asks me if I will let the group pray for me. I agree out of both courtesy and curiosity, and sit on a chair under the scripture-scribbled beams as seven near strangers gather around me. One by one they lay their hands on my shoulders, my head, my back, each hand a different temperature and pressure, each one pulsing energy through my body. I bow my head and stare at the bare foot of one of the girlfriends, fixing my eyes on the candlelight dancing off her silver toe ring. Trying to push the lyrics of Sleater-Kinney's "All Hands on the Bad One" from my mind—which I seem at this moment to be living out with awkward literalism—I breathe deeply the too-sweet scent of Gordon's vanilla candles, but I can't give myself over to the moment. The room is silent for a long time. *You can't get to heaven in your Sunday best, when the night before they were calling it your cocktail dress.* Wayne clears his throat. *All hands on the bad one.* Another jet splits the sky overhead. I wonder if it's an F-16. I wonder how scared the pilot in training must be. I can't seem to bridge the distance between myself and these hands. *All hands on the bad one.*

Gordon begins to speak. "Lord, help Lauren to form relationships quickly on her travels so she can deeply understand people in a short span of time. Help support her objectivity and lack of agenda."

Silence. Slowly my stiff back begins to soften.

Then a male voice; I think it's Tim: "Dear Lord, please lead her to the places all over the country she should go so she can tell this story the best way possible, spreading truth to her readers everywhere."

Silence. I find myself slowly relaxing into the warmth of the seven hands upon me.

A melodic female voice joins in. "Please, God, protect her car. We pray you keep her as safe as possible inside. Please make sure she has no tribulations to overcome so she can focus on her work."

Silence. My resistance melts away a bit more; all I can hear are their voices, all I can feel is their desire to ease my way.

Another female voice softly fills the room. "Dear Lord, please, when Lauren sits down to write this book, to write about all of us, please keep the goodness in her heart and the truth in her words. Let the words come to her easily, Lord, and let them be full of meaning and purpose."

Each articulation of my particular concerns—each so separate from their own—stokes embers inside my chest, the empathy, wisdom, and foresight of these prayerful men and women filling my eyes with tears. I finally understand: they want to save me just as I want to save them.

———

After Gordon prays for me, we hang out a bit, talking about his impending duties in Iraq. He's itching to fulfill his mission—his deployment date can't come fast enough. I tell him about my own travels there, when I spent time reporting in 2003, after the military claimed Baghdad but before the insurgency took hold. I don't mention that to the Iraqis I came to know and love, Gordon will be just another pig-headed crew cut, barking threatening orders, gesturing with a gun that could at any moment end their lives and sever their family's last threads of sanity, all without any penalty. I despise this war that Gordon defends so passionately as his life's calling, and I despise what he is so prepared to do there; both the physical violence he will surely inflict and the religious crusade he feels called upon to serve. Gordon and his brothers in arms represent what I believe to be the most terrifying, world-altering, and irreversible threat the Disciple Generation can deliver upon all of us, everywhere.

And yet, talking to Gordon this evening, after such a show of empathy, I can't help but feel genuine warmth toward him. In spite of all their loathsome warmongering, Gordon and his reverent community have convinced me that in their own way they are capable of translating Jesus' legacy of agape into their daily lives. Tonight they demonstrated the simple concept that powers and sustains this movement: they have shown me the kindness of strangers.

Slouching Toward Babylon

The odds are excellent that out of the tens of thousands of people who have crossed the threshold of New Life Church, I would be the least likely to convert. But picture this: about a week before Gordon and his holy warriors lay hands upon me in his basement, I'm at the Mill youth service, in the faux-bunker sanctuary. The worship band's power ballads have the congregation jumping and whirling in the aisles and in front of the stage—two thousand arms raised high, fingers outstretched, palms pulsing toward the electric sound, mouths belting out the lyrics beamed onto the overhead screen, singing to Jesus, "I was lost, I was afraid, until you found me and took me by the hand. Now I'm screaming from the top of my lungs, you are God, I know, I will shout it from the rooftops." All around me, people are literally falling to their knees and rocking back and forth.

After nearly two hours of breathless worship, the twenty-something pastor tells his flock he knows they've run overtime, and everyone is free to go, but he feels something extraordinary happening that night, and worship will continue for anyone who wants to stay. Instead of the expected class-dismissed rush to the nearest exit, the only motion is closer to the stage to sing as the drums crescendo.

By this time, I have heard the following sentence in hundreds of conversion conversations: "The worship band was playing, and suddenly I felt a brokenness inside and I couldn't stop crying." Well. The worship band is playing. Suddenly, I feel a brokenness inside. And I can't stop crying.

Despite my guardedness and my skepticism, was this to be the moment when I am born again? Has my long trip here been not my own journalistic investigation, but a path God has set to bring me to him? *Are you there, God? It's me, Lauren.* Then it hits me—of course I'm vulnerable, I have my period. And on top of that, as you've no doubt learned by now, I've been pretty aggrieved about what I've been witnessing on my journey.

So what kept me that night from becoming another Heather Erickson or Freddie Fisher? In my moment of vulnerability, had I desired to open my arms to a community of believers who would welcome me with potlucks, punk rock, and all the agape a girl could want, their ready-made package of support and certainty would have fallen into place. All I would have had to do was sign a decision card committing my life to Christ, and a whole new world would have been mine. But my hard-won self-confidence kept me sturdy under those red lights while a lifetime of classroom discussions and dinner-table discourse steeled my rational philosophy;

the volumes that line my bookshelves like sentries did not rest their defenses. But if I had been younger, teetering in my own sense of purpose, and less steeped in the literature, I have no doubt that they could have had me.

Each day during my travels through Christian America, in every living room, courtroom, or dorm room, I asked myself, *Is this for real?* as if I was trying to awaken from a baffling, endless dream.

How can teenagers turn their backs on a century and a half of science's progress? How can students at Patrick Henry College read the canon of Western philosophy and still believe that the Bible is the inerrant word of God? How can pro-life missionaries travel to see babies dying across the globe and still focus their energy to save the unborn instead of the living? How can the women of Mars Hill Church willfully submit their equal rights just one generation after feminism's Second Wave? How can members of the air force undergo training in Mesopotamia's culture and history and still believe they are delivering salvation unto the heathen world? How is all this possible when archives of dissent and critical thinking are available to anyone with Internet access? It defies reason. Literally.

Cameron Strang, the publisher of *Relevant* books and magazine, is the only person who appears in these chapters who told me he knows his faith is necessarily divorced from reason; accepting the idea of the resurrection, he says, requires a complete separation from rational thinking. Some believers work to balance an intellectual existence with what a Christian friend of mine calls "the fairy tale I picked and I'm sticking with," but almost every young Christian I've met takes the faith out of faith and replaces it with truth. It's this inscribing of authority onto belief that not only distorts faith but politicizes it. Take, for example, the faith of Clinton LeSueur, the congressional hopeful from Greenville, Mississippi, whose faith exists outside the realm of the unknowable and inside the classroom and the legislature. His faith isn't faith at all, it's the perception of absolute truth, a truth LeSueur wants to do more than *speak* to power, or even *fight* the power—he wants it to *be* the power.

A particularly cerebral friend of mine is a young and impossibly blond Evangelical Texan named Jason Boyett, who writes books and a magazine column for *Relevant*. In an aphorism typical of his clear-eyed perspective, Jason condemns LeSueur and other absolutists in his generation of Christians: "Faith as certainty is a fascist's attitude." He likes to tell the story that opens Stephen Hawking's *A Brief History of Time*, about a woman who, at a public lecture on astronomy, announced she thought the world was perched on the back of a turtle. When the scientist giving the lecture asked her smugly what she thought the turtle was standing on, she replied, "It's turtles all the way down." Jason is the son of voracious readers, and became one himself at an early age; he credits reading with maintaining his faith as *faith*—knowing he believes to a certain extent that "it's turtles all the way down"—instead of the truth-or-lies Manichaeism that colors so much of contemporary Christianity.

"Christians fear education," Jason says, "because it shows you the gray areas. The more I read outside my subculture, the more the black-and-white of the Bible becomes submerged." Jason's faith is a process of examining himself and his God; he chooses to live by the parts of the Bible that benefit humanity, and after careful philosophical scrutiny, disregards the rest. Still, if I gathered together Jason, Gordon, Rock for Life's Erik Whittington, they'd all find they have far more in common than not; the faith they share unites them beyond any of their own intellectual or aesthetic differences. It's not just faith that aligns them, but an overarching worldview and a mutual purpose: they are united to save souls for Christ. Together and individually, they are *called.*

"Calling," Jason explains to me over Tex-Mex one afternoon, "is a question of lifestyle instead of a crisis response." We're talking about his brother, Brooks, a twenty-nine-year-old with sandy hair and a face that wouldn't look out of place in the pages of an Abercrombie catalog. Brooks was making great money working in finance and marketing until a couple of years ago, when he says he "started feeling a burden for the poor." He couldn't shake a feeling he thought was coming from God, so he read the gospels and tried to figure out what his Lord was telling him to do. One day he paid a visit to a church in the toughest neighborhood in Amarillo and asked if he could volunteer once a week in their program to feed poor kids. He started that evening, splitting and serving ears of corn on the cob, when a nine-year-old girl approached him to ask for another helping, and for paper towels and a sack so she could take it home to feed her hungry family. As Brooks looked into her huge dark eyes, he swears he heard the voice of God talking to him. "It wasn't like a talking fish or the voice of James Earl Jones," he tells me, "it was a voice that came from deep inside me saying, *Once a week is not enough*."

Brooks went home that night and read Matthew 25:40, in which Jesus says, "Inasmuch as you did it to one of the least of these my brethren, you did it to me." He immediately quit his job and founded Mission 2540, where he now works with more than two hundred kids. I first met Brooks when Jason took me to a birthday party he was throwing in a housing project, which is what he does when he's not filling new backpacks with school supplies, helping children deal with home lives that are rife with violence, and leading kids' study groups on themes like "Famous Fights of the Bible." At sunset one night we drove out to Groom, Texas, to see what is said to be the largest cross in the Western Hemisphere, looming tall and white over the prairie. In the car, Brooks told me that the Mission 2540 is his reason to be on earth, period—not his lovely young wife or his button-cute kids. "Many days I don't want to be doing this. But like Paul said, Jesus Christ compels me. There's no way I'd be doing this without my faith," he said. "I could know it's something I *should* be doing, but without God I'd just ask, *Well, why?*"

In a synergy that fails to surprise me anymore, Brooks is one of many social-welfare-minded urban missionaries who votes Republican. He is the Disciple Generation equivalent of the sixties kids who renounced consumerism and careerism to join the antiwar movement, the Peace Corps, the union organizers when hundreds of thousands of people in that generation felt called into service—*if you weren't part of the solution you were part of the problem*. But those days saw the influence of secular—albeit God-fearing—leaders who stimulated a commitment to something greater than themselves, like the holy trinity of MLK, JFK, and RFK, each of whom, once assassinated, was never to be replaced. In Brooks's generation, there's a leader who can never be gunned down on a hotel balcony, or in a convertible, or at a podium in the ballroom of a Los Angeles hotel; a leader who provides authority, agape, and the will to make change. It's hard to imagine anything in our leaderless secular society that can begin to compete with the guidance found in Jesus Christ.

Ultimately, though, the calling to beneficence of guys like Brooks Boyett, or Ted Bruun and his Extreme Tour missionaries, or even the fame-spurning members of Goodside in no way separates them from the army of Evangelicals with designs on your soul. For all their oblation, one must not overlook the fact that the Disciple Generation is foremost a growing fundamentalist population. The apocalyptic imagination, the annihilation of the individual, the subjugation of women, the resistance to competing ideas—all these startling facets of this movement are conventional aspects of fundamentalism of any kind, anywhere.

Likewise, the symptoms of our society that give rise to this fundamentalism are akin to what exists wherever fundamentalist movements take root. As Karen Armstrong writes in *Islam: A Short History*, "Fundamentalist movements in all faiths share certain characteristics. They reveal a deep disappointment and disenchantment with the modern experience, that has not fulfilled all that it promised"—words that could be lifted from the diary of any Disciple Generation member.

We need only look eastward to see how fundamentalism can gather its angry power, fanning jihadist rage under the daily threat of violence in Baghdad or Gaza, as fear mounts and spreads.

Whether they are living in a region gutted by war, or in a banality-riddled nation like our own, the experience of modernity for many people is a lifetime of loneliness, the ache of utter isolation in an impossibly huge and uncaring world. It is a cocktail of fear and loneliness that brings people to the door of a church (or a mosque), or that encourages receptivity to the words of a skate pastor (or a madrasa teacher). Fundamentalism offers a snake-oil cure for their ills, promising the tight community groups of churches, the steadfast solidarity of activist groups, and most of all, the deep certainty of biblical inerrancy. The ache of modernity, as Hannah Arendt wrote in *The Origins of Totalitarianism*, is a great enabler of the rise of fascism, which "bases itself on loneliness, on the experience of not belonging to the world at all, which is among the most radical and desperate experiences of man." Furthermore, Arendt remarked that "in this situation man loses trust in himself as the partner of his thoughts," a symptom that is clear in the Disciple Generation's triumvirate of emotion, politics, and anti-intellectualism, even what Arendt called the "extreme contempt for facts."

Although on the road I often recalled what a priest in Germany warned journalist Dorothy Thompson in 1934— "That is their program, to get the children"—I do not mean to assert that the Disciple Generation is the next Nazi Party; I'll happily leave the swastika drawing to the mysterious hand that defaced my dusty car at Cornerstone. But we cannot underestimate the lessons of history: it's no overstatement to declare that there is a tyranny over the hearts and minds of this generation, which is swiftly being exported abroad. Gordon Harrell's insistent doublespeak that his fundamentalism *is* freedom, and that his job is to spread freedom throughout the world, should be an alarm sounding to all of us, religious or secular.

The very founding ethic of this country is the liberty to live how one wants, no matter how much a movement of Christian fundamentalists strives to obscure that essential principle, while cloaking itself in the American flag. Whether or not the Founding Fathers were Christians, and regardless of what Michael Farris tells his students, this nation was established to ensure that belief was private and protected, not along the lines of *There is but one God* but *Ain't nobody's business if you do*. My anxiety about the rising tide of evangelism is not generated by people's duly protected *beliefs*; it's a response to people's *deeds*. To borrow again from Arendt, in a time of tyranny people do not *think*, they *act*.

Arendt's comrades in the Old Left may have been able to envision a futuristic state in which a Christian youth movement rallies around a right-wing agenda transmitted via podcasts— it's a dystopian scenario straight out of the satires that were written in opposition to totalitarianism. But I'm willing to bet members of the sixties New Left could have never dreamed they'd see their own cultural tactics achieving mass outreach on the Christian right, nor could they have imagined how inclusive a revolution could be. The Disciple Generation—whether you're an air force cadet or a hemp-clad vegan—cuts across demographic lines in a way that's usually contrary to revolution; certainly it was in the sixties. The true radicals knew whom they wanted alongside them on the front lines, and that scope didn't include suburban housewives hot for beaded curtains and mother's little helper pills. The difference between revolutionaries and people who were merely wrapped up in a lifestyle trend was, to quote Stephen Baldwin, the answer to the question *Are you livin it?*

Ordinarily, the more that radicalism crosses over into different social spheres, the more it dilutes, until it's not all that radical anymore. But the New Left was even more self-selecting than its antiestablishment politics would suggest, especially the left that prevailed after bus trips south to the Delta had subsided and the Summer of Love had come and gone. For example, turning on and dropping out of the capitalist cycle tended to be the luxury of kids with a fall-back plan, just in case they need to opt out of opting out; eschewing money is a bourgeois affect. And why would blacks who had nothing but the rights they acquired at the end of a fire hose reject their new possibility of prosperity? Leftists, in their all-out battle against consumerism and the establishment, made enemies who would prove to be great uniters across class, race, and culture, members of a mainstream that in time would swing far to the right.

John Patrick Diggins wrote in *Rise and Fall of the American Left*, "the Left has always identified itself in opposition to the actual state of things." Today, the left doesn't even seem to recognize the actual state of things. The amassing Disciple Generation goes unnoticed as a, if not *the*, primary agent of change in our country. For all the hand-wringing about religiosity today—*Should we take on religion as part of our platforms, too?* so many Democratic strategists deliberate—it's not only the movement itself that is largely ignored, but also the social symptoms that have delivered us this Christian army. I am reminded of Jesus' frustration with his own disciples. "You can discern the face of the sky and of the earth," he said, "but how is it you do not discern this time?"

It seems that almost no one acknowledges the course of this underground civil war. The only people aware of it are the ones deep in its trenches: the soldiers of the salvation army, steadily spreading the gospel of their conservative politics every day. They look around them and see a world of nonbelievers, all of us *dogs and sorcerers and sexually immoral and murderers and idolaters*, as John wrote in Revelation. We look around and what do we see? People who look like us. It's time for the left to open its eyes to the actual state of things, to look below the surface, to feel *called*. It's time to mount an opposition.

The Disciple Generation continuously multiplies and thrives because the secular left can't even find the words to express why life is worth living; we can't even play the game. But just as the left of the sixties inadvertently taught the religious right of today how to connect culture, politics, and community to galvanize a movement, we can learn from how Evangelicals reach out and organize today. In fact, the left has always done well sampling from the Christian realm: without Christianity there would have been no organized movements for abolition, women's suffrage, or civil rights. Whether or not I believe in Marx's mass-opiate adage more than I believe in

God, I can see the extraordinary humanism at the heart of most religion, with its undeniable promise of connection to something extraordinary.

The question remains, can we actually win this fight without God? In a society full of questions and hungry for answers, rising tides of supplicants have determined that the only place those answers—that *certainty*—lies is in Christianity, since, more often than not, that's the only assurance they're being sold. The secular world has left a vacuum yawning in modernity's barren atmosphere; it's the most zealous "called" Christian candidates who have rushed in to fill it. As a consequence, the risk of Christian extremists dictating life in this country is a very, very real possibility: the foundation has already been laid. This is scary. But within these menacing words, there is some optimism to be found. People are eagerly searching; they are open and receptive.

That's why I'm preaching, as much as it makes my skin crawl to do so. In our secular world, we must recognize the same hunger for meaning that Christians do, and we must respond by lacing our television shows, newspapers and magazines, university dialogue, and political discourse with a greater sense of life's value, all with enough humor, style, and rock 'n' roll to make it palatable; a teaspoon of irony to help the medicine go down. It's madness that to live a life of meaning, one would be required to swear that a man was resurrected from the dead two thousand years ago, and that his dad created the earth a few thousand years before that. Obviously, plenty of us secularists build our own purpose-driven lives without God, but for people who have a tough time figuring out how, they shouldn't have to swap faith in the material world for the promise of meaning and community. If faith is something you truly feel—if you really do believe that it's "turtles all the way down"—fine, whatever gets you through the night is all right. I can't help but wonder, though, how many people have convinced themselves they believe, just to experience the benefits of being a believer. To whatever extent we can, secularists must offer what the Christian world promises, so that whenever someone signs a pledge—literally or figuratively—that the Bible is the inerrant word of God, they're doing so only because their faith has led them to that conclusion, and not their desperation.

Instead of teaching, as they do in Colorado Springs and all over the nation, that a beast covered in eyes will usher in happiness after the earth has been left behind, we need to help lift people out of their own personal hells to find some heaven on earth. To compete with Christian culture, we may need to develop a more Christian apparatus, much as they have co-opted the rock festivals and skate parks of the secular world. It's time to consider secular counterparts to parachurches like Acquire the Fire, home church groups like the Dietzes', major institutions like New Life, and traveling experiments like the Extreme Tour. Some models exist already, but we need many more.

We need our own Rock for Life at our own Cornerstones vibrating with our own music that takes a stand. We need our own Patrick Henry Colleges connecting higher education to political upheaval, drawing from an activist base of teenagers grown out of our own Generation Joshua. We need our own *Purpose-Driven Life* that will inspire people to action and offer them a reason for living. We need to cultivate our own networks of fence builders, and our own platoons of authentically cool skaters reaching out to kids searching for identity and belonging. We need a culture that says more, that demands more, that expects more. We need people who want to compete, and we have to make them ourselves, not by creating automatons who will utter rote statements, but by returning to the simple Platonic notion that the unexamined life is not worth living. We have to inculcate a generation—and beyond—with the desire to believe in more than personal gain, so the cultural machinery we develop for activism, education, and support will be where they want to devote time, money, and hearts.

Our culture needs to offer something more than mere escapism. Christians making their own culture today are circumventing the massive corporations that get richer and richer off cheaper and cheaper thrills; secularists need to participate in a greater push to connect culture with meaning outside the corporate sphere, since it will never occur inside it. I'm hardly the first to point out the fact that corporations have replaced our institutions, engorged more every day on the fat of rampant consumerism. The Disciple Generation rebels against a soulless corporate structure. Like the sixties generation that came before it, it blames the system, but today the system it blames isn't the government, but the conglomerates. As secularism becomes synonymous with the corporate sphere—in the eyes of Christians and non-Christians alike—a David and Goliath struggle has emerged between corporations and communities, which is won these days only when communities have a church to keep them organized and strong.

It is time for our own secular Great Awakening. It's up to us to do what Jesus would do, to reach out to those who believe we are the enemy, to lift up the poor and needy, and to turn the world on its head as he did. Jesus said to his disciples, " 'He is like a man building a house, who dug deep and laid the foundation on the rock. And when the flood arose, the stream beat vehemently against that house, and could not shake it, for it was founded on the rock. But he who heard and did nothing is like a man who built a house on the earth without a foundation against which the stream beat vehemently; and immediately it fell. And the ruin of that house is great.' " This need not be our own end of days; we must rebuild our broken home with bricks of reason, under a roof of agape, and upon a foundation of enlightenment rock-hard enough to withstand the flood to come.

Acknowledgments

I am continuously amazed, no matter where I travel or what I write about, to find how generous people can be with their stories and their time. I thank every person I interviewed in reporting this book, none of whom asked anything of me—except to save my soul, but that's what you get when you embark on a project like this one. Along with the people I interviewed, I read dozens of books in researching this book, and I am particularly indebted to the scholarship and analysis of Mark Noll, William McLoughlin, and Richard Hofstader.

My researchers worked for nothing but trouble: Michael O'Connell kept me going on the road and back home in Brooklyn with his whip-smart mind and effervescent humor, Gerald Helland helped with some initial research for the book, and Jonathan Morgan assembled the index of statistics from heaps of numbers he found. I am also indebted to Michael Kiser in Virginia and Shelly Jennings in Seattle, two very special and invaluable people to meet while I was coordinating my reporting.

On the road, a number of people gave me respite from the endless procession of Super 8 motels: Adrienne Schure in Denver, the Roarks in Atlanta, the Jensens in Raleigh, the Boyetts in Amarillo, my girl Lia Bonfilio in Chicago, and Jethro Heiko and Chelsea Thompson in Philly. Jeff and Cami Zelevansky offered wine and a bed when the car broke down in Jersey fifteen miles into a six-thousand-mile road trip, and my fairy godmother Susan Garsoe and Tim Davis provided heavenly pie and killer social insight in Colorado Springs.

Several dear friends read sections or early drafts, and I would have been at sea without their encouragement, notably Vanessa Mobley, Kate Bolick, Jeff Howe, Carlene Bauer, Eric Hynes, Lauren Kaminsky, Sarah Spitz, Mark Bauer, Katie Meier, and Diana Jensen—David Matthews endured multiple drafts of my book even while deep into his own, and was always available for neurotic phone calls and dinner breaks. I'm blessed with many friends who extended additional support, especially Jeff Cohen and Justine Wiltshire, Erika Kawalek and Tyler Maroney, Alysia Abbott, Adam Higginbotham, and Leslie Koren.

At Viking, I thank my editor, Molly Stern, art director Paul Buckley, copy editor Chuck Antony, and rising star Alessandra Lusardi. My agent, Amy Williams, defines fierce anew, even when she's nine months pregnant.

Most formidably, I am grateful to my family, including my grandparents, who continue to bolster me, and Jon and Terry Lane, who challenge and cherish me as only true family can. My parents, James and Judith Sandler, sent me off to summer camp with a T-shirt they made that said,

QUESTION AUTHORITY BUT NOT YOUR MOTHER—their support and ideals motivate and anchor my work every day. And most of all, I thank Justin Lane, my husband and partner in work and adventure, who brought both his camera and his sound perspective on the road with me to capture this slice of America. Justin embodies all the agape a girl could need; without him, this book—and my life—would be a paltry thing indeed.